The West Side of Any Mountain

The West Side

of Any Mountain

Place, Space, and Ecopoetry

J. Scott Bryson

University of Iowa Press | Iowa City

University of Iowa Press, Iowa City 52242
http://www.uiowa.edu/uiowapress
Copyright © 2005 by the University of Iowa Press
All rights reserved
Printed in the United States of America
Design by April Leidig-Higgins

A shorter version of chapter 3 appeared in the Fall 2002 issue (27.3) of *MELUS: Multi-Ethnic Literature of the United States.* Used with permission.

Chapter 5 is an extended version of an essay that originally appeared in *Ecopoetry: A Critical Introduction*, J. Scott Bryson, ed. (Salt Lake City: University of Utah Press, 2002). Used with permission.

The University of Iowa Press is a member of Green Press Initiative and is committed to preserving natural resources.

Printed on acid-free paper

Library of Congress Cataloging-in-Publication Data
Bryson, J. Scott, 1968–.
The west side of any mountain: place, space, and ecopoetry / by J. Scott Bryson.
    p.   cm.
    Includes bibliographical references (p.   ) and index.
ISBN 0-87745-955-x (cloth)
1. American poetry—20th century—History and criticism.
2. Nature in literature.   3. Merwin, W. S. (William Stanley),
1927– —Criticism and interpretation.   4. Berry, Wendell, 1934–
—Criticism and interpretation.   5. Oliver, Mary, 1935– —
Criticism and interpretation.   6. Harjo, Joy—Criticism and
interpretation.   7. Place (Philosophy) in literature.   8. Space
and time in literature.   9. Ecology in literature.   I. Title.
PS310.N3B79 2005
811'.540936—dc22   2005047011

05 06 07 08 09 C 5 4 3 2 1

For T

Contents

The West Side of Any Mountain

Preface

AS ECOCRITICISM exploded onto the critical scene during the 1990s, and fascinating and important work was produced that allowed us to view significant literary artists in new and greener light, *poets* writing from an environmental perspective received relatively little critical attention. Until fairly recently, granting certain exceptions, ecocritical scholars have focused almost exclusively on fiction and nonfiction, examining the works of prose nature writers like Thoreau, Leopold, Dillard, and Abbey. However, the pioneering critical work on contemporary nature poetry produced by John Elder, Terry Gifford, and Patrick Murphy has recently been followed up in studies by Gyorgyi Voros, Leonard Scigaj, Jonathan Bate, Bernard W. Quetchenbach, and David Gilcrest.[1] This book's main purpose is to participate in and further the initial wave of scholarly attention paid to contemporary nature poetry, much of which has come to be called "ecopoetry," and to offer a theoretical apparatus with which to interact more fully with this dynamic and increasingly significant field of literature.

Although the term "ecopoetry" seems to be acquiring a certain amount of critical momentum, a definitive name for the current environmentally aware version of nature poetry has not been clearly established. And while a remarkable synergy exists among scholars exploring the field, an authoritative definition has not yet appeared either. Recent critics in particular, however, have attempted to define the new brand of nature poetry. Gifford assigns the term "green poetry" to "those recent nature poems which engage directly with environmental issues" (3). And Scigaj writes that we "might define ecopoetry as poetry that persistently stresses human cooperation with nature conceived as a dynamic, interrelated series of cyclic feedback systems" (37). He distinguishes ecopoetry from what he calls "environmental poetry," which "reveres nature and often focuses on particular environmental issues, but without the ecopoet's particular concentration on nature as an interrelated series of cyclic feedback systems" (37).[2] Lawrence Buell sets down overarching characteristics of "environmentally oriented works" in general—the presence of the nonhuman as more than mere backdrop, the expansion of human interest beyond humanity, a sense of human accountability to the environment and of the environment as a process rather than a constant or given—and these characteristics presumably apply to poetry as well (7–8). And Murphy includes, in his taxonomy of "American nature-oriented literature," a category of poetry that meets his criteria of "environmental literature," which, among other things, "advocates political and ethical values" regarding humans and their interaction with nature (*FA* 2). Finally, Gilcrest distinguishes "ecological poetry" from both contemporary nature poetry and traditional romantic poetry, and he characterizes it as typified by a critique of "atomistic and mechanistic . . . conceptual schemas"; an identification of an environmental crisis based on those schemas; "an appeal to revolutionary transformations" based on ecological science; and the origin of "an ecocentric ethic of interconnectedness, reciprocity, and, in some instances, radical egalitarianism" (24).

In my introduction to the 2002 edited collection *Ecopoetry: A Critical Introduction*, I attempted to offer a definition that summarizes this earlier ecocritical work on ecopoetry, condensing the overall characterization of the mode so as to spotlight both the similarities and the differences between ecopoetry and what most people expect when they encounter conventional lyrical nature poetry. As a (still tentative) definition, I asserted that ecopoetry is a mode that, while adhering to certain conventions of traditional nature poetry, advances beyond that tradition and takes on distinctly contemporary problems and issues, thus becoming generally marked by three primary characteristics: an ecological and biocentric perspective recognizing the interdependent nature of the world; a deep humility with regard to our relationships with human and nonhuman nature; and an intense skepticism toward hyperrationality, a skepticism that usually leads to condemnation of an overtechnologized modern world and a warning concerning the very real potential for ecological catastrophe.

These attributes characterize ecopoetry as a mode that both connects with and diverges from earlier versions of nature poetry. While ecopoems are indeed simply the latest in a long line of nature poetry, they also are in some ways a new type of poem, a new movement in poetry, one that seeks to stir readers to action in new ways. As Scigaj explains, ecopoets "want the poem to challenge and reconfigure the reader's perceptions so to put the book down and live life more fully in all possible dimensions of the moment of firsthand experience within nature's supportive second skin and to become more responsible about that necessary second skin" (41). Granted, ecopoetic lines, and even entire ecopoems, have been written by many poets who precede the modern environmental movement yet still demonstrate the general characteristics associated with ecopoetry. In other words, it is not the case, of course, that for the first time in modern history poems are being produced that recognize reciprocity within nature and seek to interact humbly with all of the natural world. However, the widespread emphasis on ecology within contemporary intellectual circles *is* a relatively new occurrence, and the difference in terms of verse is that ecopoets are aiming at a poetics that presents the world community as just that, a *community*, rather than a world of creatures and natural beings with whom the privileged human self interacts. Indeed, the justification and need for this type of exhortation is what is really new, as we are faced with environmental crises that humans have not previously faced, and could hardly have imagined, in recorded history, crises that proceed out of a lost awareness of what the Mohawk poet Peter Blue Cloud has called the "allness of the creation." Generally speaking, then, ecopoetry has emerged as a historical phenomenon arising from particular circumstances.

As I discuss in the chapters to follow, many ecopoets write out of a self-consciousness that helps them (at least partially) avoid the charge leveled against romantics in general and many environmentalists in particular, that they seem to know that the loss of relationship with the natural world is irrevocable, yet they continue to call for some sort of healing of that breach. What we'll see is that ecopoets are indeed intensely aware of that loss and its permanence, and they certainly continue to yearn for the relationship. However, the important distinction here lies in the poets' awareness of the impossibility of a literal return to old ways. This issue will be the focus of chapter 1, where I discuss the synergism between the concepts of place and space, as articulated by the cultural geographer Yi-Fu Tuan. I turn then to four individual poets—Wendell Berry, Joy Harjo, Mary Oliver, and W. S. Merwin—in terms of three primary objectives: (1) to examine each poet's response to the modern, dualistic split between human and nonhuman nature; (2) to explore each writer's poetry in light of the Tuanian place-space framework set up in chapter 1; and (3) to discuss the framework itself in terms of its usefulness and effectiveness at analyzing, critiquing, and comparing different ecopoets.

These chapters proceed thematically, rather than chronologically. Rather than moving sequentially from Merwin to Berry to Oliver to Harjo, I proceed according to how each poet presents and interacts with the concepts of place and space. To be more specific, juxtaposing these four authors demonstrates that each of them displays a keen awareness of a connection to place as I'm defining it here. In their articulation of the attitudes associated with a Tuanian space-consciousness, however, they subtly but significantly differ, with these distinctions centering primarily on how each poet views language and its relationship to poetry and nature, how each poet recognizes, in Gilcrest's words, "the border between language and the living world as a frontier beyond which abides the truly wild" (148).

Chapter 2 focuses on Berry, whose readers will witness his awareness of place and space as well as the moments when language lets him down as he attempts to communicate his values, for instance, in his reliance on the problematically dualistic civilization/wilderness vocabulary. Chapter 3 examines the work of Harjo, who in her discussion of place and space makes explicit the problematic nature of language in terms of its ability to render her experiences with the world around her; however, she appears more inclined to blame the Western, English language she has inherited, rather than language itself. She therefore looks to discover the means to "go back" to a time and place of nonduality and relational significance. Chapter 4 looks at Oliver's self-conscious awareness of the way she uses words and rhetorical tropes, in particular the pathetic fallacy, and the way her self-reflexive use of language connects her to the nonhuman world while reminding her (and her readers) of her ultimate separation from it. Chapter 5 explores Merwin and his fundamental anxiety regarding language and its inadequacies; as a result of this unease, Merwin uses words to let go of words, relies on language to overcome his reliance on language, and ultimately (or, at least often) decides that as a result of his own self-consciousness, he has nothing to say at all.

I have selected these poets to demonstrate the highly divergent voices at work within the mode. I could have chosen countless others, among them Gary Snyder, Leslie Marmon Silko, Denise Levertov, James Wright, Simon Ortiz, Arthur Sze, and A. R. Ammons, to name only a few. Yet a juxtaposition of Berry, Harjo, Oliver, and Merwin offers the opportunity to ask unique questions concerning the usefulness of the place-space framework in interacting with ecological texts.

Finally, I want to acknowledge those who have contributed to my personal and intellectual development and have therefore directly or indirectly influenced this book. First, I am grateful to my parents for their lifelong love and encouragement, and for lessons that significantly affected my relationship with ecopoetry. Mom and Bill have taught me the interrelationship between being and searching, showing me the importance of home and place as well as the glory of ignorance and space. And Dad, my trusted proofreader and unquestioned supporter, has not only instructed me in the importance of roots and family, but also introduced me to the invaluable space-centered principle that "you can't whup everybody that needs whupping, and you can't eat all the ice cream." I am also grateful to my brother Chris, for his friendship and for the model he provides of a life lived with purpose and principles.

I also want to thank my two primary academic mentors, Dana Nelson and Steve Weisenburger. Over the last few years they have taken time to advise me on not only academic and scholarship matters but career and personal issues as well, and they have done so graciously during extremely busy times for each of them. Moreover, Dana was the first to show enthusiasm for this project and has encouraged me throughout, while Steve influenced me early in my doctoral studies by demonstrating, in the several courses I took with him, what a true scholar is. Both have been unwavering encouragers and honest critics of my work.

Lastly, I acknowledge my friend and partner and wife, Tina Payne Bryson, to whom this book is dedicated. Although I might have been able to complete it without her help and support, I wouldn't have had nearly as much fun doing it. I am grateful to her for the many walks and road trips and ping-pong games during which she listened to me ramble on about ideas only marginally interesting to her; for helping me hone those ideas for clarity; and for being always supportive. I greatly respect and admire her, and I thank her for the gifts of Ben and Luke.

CHAPTER ONE

All Finite Things Reveal Infinitude | Place, Space, and Contemporary Ecopoetry

What we require, then, is neither disparagement nor celebration of place-sense but an account of those specific conditions under which it significantly furthers . . . environmental humility, an awakened place-awareness that is also mindful of its limitations and respectful that place molds us as well as vice versa.

—Lawrence Buell, *The Environmental Imagination*

IN A 1998 ARTICLE in the *New Yorker*, Jerry Brown answered a question about his move to Oakland by saying:

> Cheap land. I wanted to build a live-work facility. I wanted to live in a grittier place than San Francisco. That's a problem today: people don't live in place, they live in space. The media used to accuse *me* of that—living in space. But it wasn't true. Now too many people just live in their minds, not in communities. They garage themselves in their homes and live in market space. It's an alienated way for human beings to live. It's the difference between a native and an immigrant. A native lives in place, not space. Without roots, there is no morality.

Brown's position—that humans need to reconnect with a sense of place, rather than living in some sort of abstract (cyber- or market-) space—is familiar within environmental circles, where the concept of "place" is discussed a great deal these days.[1] And while the essence of his statement is certainly in keeping with much current environmental sentiment, it also demonstrates a key linguistic disorientation regarding the terms "place" and "space," a confusion that often appears in references to contemporary nature poetry (and, indeed, to most forms of nature writing). A primary objective of this book is to problematize this bias toward place and against space, demonstrating the usefulness and importance of understanding the significant and interdependent relationship between the two terms. Having done so, we can use these relational terms to attain a fuller understanding of developments in what is coming to be called ecopoetry.

Put simply, ecopoets offer a vision of the world that values the interaction between two interdependent and seemingly paradoxical desires, both of which are attempts to respond to the modern divorce between humanity and the rest of nature: (1) to *create place*, making a conscious and concerted effort to know the more-than-human world around us; and (2) to *value space*, recognizing the extent to which that very world is ultimately unknowable. Without being overly rigid, I want to suggest that most of the project undertaken by contemporary ecopoets falls somewhere within these two objectives, to know the world and to recognize its ultimate unknowability. Using the work of the cultural geographer Yi-Fu Tuan, along with other thinkers from different disciplines, we can come to a clearer understanding of the concepts of "place" and "space" and the way they relate to contemporary ecopoetry.

IN HIS LANDMARK *Space and Place: The Perspective of Experience,* Tuan explains that the concepts "space" and "place" "require each other for definition. From security and stability of place we are aware of the openness, freedom, and threat of space, and vice versa. Furthermore, if we think of space as that which allows movement, then place is pause; each pause in movement makes it possible for location to be transformed into place" (6). Place and space are therefore interdependent and necessary for a full and healthy vision of the world around us. These key Tuanian concepts offer the means to better comprehend what ecopoets are doing in their work.

First, before examining space, the lesser-discussed component of the dichotomy, let's consider the concept of place and its relation to ecopoetry. As Tuan puts it, " 'Space' is more abstract than 'place.' What begins as undifferentiated space becomes place as we get to know it better and endow it with value" (6). For example, a neighborhood "is at first a confusion of images to the new resident; it is blurred space 'out there.' Learning to know the neighborhood requires the identification of significant localities, such as street corners and architectural landmarks, within the neighborhood space" (17–18). Thus, "enclosed and humanized space is place" (54), for "place is a type of object. Places and objects define space, giving it a geometric personality. Neither the newborn infant nor the man who gains sight after a lifetime of blindness can immediately recognize a geometric shape such as a triangle. The triangle is at first 'space,' a blurred image. Recognizing the triangle requires the prior identification of corners—that is, places" (17).[2]

One way to apply Tuan's definition of place to the work of ecopoets is to view the writers as similar to what the linguistic anthropologist Keith Basso calls "place-makers," the Western Apache storytellers with whom he has lived and worked. In his latest work, *Wisdom Sits in Places,* Basso explains that these place-makers, in the stories they tell their audiences, create what he calls imaginative "place-worlds" that serve as alternate conceptions of how the world could be. According to Basso, Western Apache place-makers "fashion possible worlds, give them expressive shape, and present them for

Place, Space, and Contemporary Ecopoetry | 9

contemplation as images of the past that can deepen and enlarge awareness of the present" (*WSP* 32). Serving as tribal historians, these place-makers actually create place in the minds of their listeners by relating the old stories, always rooted in the surrounding landscape:

> For Indian men and women, the past lies embedded in features of the earth — in canyons and lakes, mountains and arroyos, rocks and vacant fields — which together endow their lands with multiple forms of significance that reach into their lives and shape the ways they think. Knowledge of places is therefore closely linked to knowledge of the self, to grasping one's position in the larger scheme of things, including one's own community, and to securing a confident sense of who one is as a person. (*WSP* 34)

In other words, in offering stories from the past, the storytellers create worlds before the eyes of the audience, worlds that can serve as both alternatives and models for those living in the present. "In the country of the past, as Apaches like to explore it, the place-maker is an indispensable guide" (*WSP* 32), because, as Basso puts it,

> every developed place-world manifests itself as a possible state of affairs, and whenever these constructions are accepted by other people as credible and convincing — or plausible and provocative, or arresting and intriguing — they enrich the common stock on which everyone can draw to muse on past events, interpret their significance and imagine them anew. Building and sharing place — worlds, in other words, is not only a means of reviving former times but also of *revising* them, a means of exploring not merely how things might have been but also how, just possibly, they might have been different from what others have supposed. Augmenting and enhancing conceptions of the past, innovative place-worlds change these conceptions as well. (*WSP* 6)

Thus, as they create their place-worlds, these place-makers offer new visions of how things have been and, implicitly, how things might be.

This role that Western Apache storytellers play for their society is similar to the one ecopoets attempt to fulfill in theirs. That is, when viewed through the lenses of Basso and Tuan, ecopoets are also often place-makers, attempting to move their audience out of an existence in an abstract postmodernized space, where we are simply visitors in an unknown neighborhood, and into a recognition of our present surroundings as place and thus as home; the goal would be to create a feeling of what Tuan calls "topophilia": "the affective bond between people and place or setting" (*Two Essays* 4). Robinson Jeffers urges topophilia and place-making when he exhorts us to "fall in love outwards," just as Pattiann Rogers makes place when she conveys the amazement with which she views flowers, insects, and small animals in a prairie, then follows that description with the question, "Whoever said *the ordinary, the mundane, / the commonplace*? Show them to me" (209). When poets offer these declarations and ask these questions, they are making place, challenging us to cease being what John Graves calls "the wearers out and movers on" (176), and instead to slow our pace and view our own surroundings as places rather than empty, spacious, unknown locations.

A related similarity between ecopoets and Western Apache place-makers comes in connection with a process Basso dubs "interanimation" and describes this way:

> As places animate the ideas and feelings of persons who attend to them, these same ideas and feelings animate the places on which attention has been bestowed, and the movements of this process—inward toward facets of the self, outward toward aspects of the external world, alternately both together—cannot be known in advance. When places are actively sensed, the physical landscape becomes wedded to the landscape of the mind, to the roving imagination, and where the mind may lead is anybody's guess. ("WSP" 55)

It is this process of interanimation, of recognizing the interdependent nature of the relationship between people and the worlds they inhabit, that enables place-making, whether it is practiced by Western Apache storytellers or contemporary U.S. nature poets.

Scott Slovic discusses this point in reference to Wendell Berry. Describing a scene in which Berry tells of looking at bluebells through a 15× lens, Slovic writes:

Closer and closer the writer examines his place, only to realize ever more powerfully that his senses alone will not complete his homecoming. What he must finally realize is that he and the inhuman inhabitants of the place are there together, participating together in the life of the place. As time passes, he begins to perceive not only the natural world as being distinct from himself, but its relationship to him, so that he concludes the essay implying continued movement and change, with the sentence: "We [the writer and an old sycamore] are moving in a relationship, a design, that is definite—though shadowy to me—like people in a dance" ([*LLH*] 55). (Slovic 127)

Examples of this type of place-making abound within ecopoetry, where time and again we see poets instructing us to recognize Silko's "spider-webbed" quality of the world, in which everything is connected to everything else. Emily Dickinson was making place when she wrote,

Some keep the Sabbath going to Church—
I keep it staying at Home—
With a Bobolink for my Chorister—
And an Orchard, for a Dome—

Likewise, Robert Bly is a place-maker when, in his prose poem "Sitting on Some Rocks in Shaw Cove," he declares that "the rocks with their backs turned to me have something spiritual in them. On these rocks I am not afraid of death; death is like the sound of the motor in an airplane as we fly, the sound so steady and comforting" (*WHI* 23). And Harjo is place-making when she writes, "Remember you are all people and all people are you. / Remember you are this universe and this universe is you" (*SHSH* 40). Berry, Silko, Dickinson, Bly, Harjo: While these writers would be considered eco-poets only to varying degrees, all are making place when they help reorient us within our world, when they render their conceptions of the world in such a way that their poems become models for how to approach the land-scape surrounding us so that we view it as meaningful place rather than ab-stract space. In other words, ecopoets encourage us to discover and nurture a topophiliac devotion to the places we inhabit. It is this type of thinking that has led to the term "inhabitation literature," used to describe nature writing.

Many times this desire to make place is transformed into a condemnation of the "placelessness" most modern Western people endure, often without any awareness of it. This placelessness is similar to T. S. Eliot's "deracination," or uprootedness, and it is characterized by what Morris Berman called alienated "disenchantment." Berman argues that modern "scientific consciousness"

> is alienated consciousness: there is no ecstatic merger with nature, but rather total separation from it. Subject and object are always seen in opposition to each other. I am not my experiences, and thus not really a part of the world around me. The logical end point of this world view is a feeling of total reification: everything is an object, alien, not-me; and I am an object too, an alienated "thing" in a world of other, equally meaningless things. (2–3)

To be placeless does not mean, of course, that a person does not exist within a literal place, but rather that that place offers nothing to the person in terms of community or belonging. A placeless person, in other words, feels little connection to his or her surroundings and thus lives in ignorance of the interanimated nature of the world.

This criticism may come in the form of a humorous statement about the ignorance of place-knowledge, as in this statement from an interview with Alberto Rios:

> There are some icons in the Southwest that point out a lack of understanding [of place]. I think particularly of the patio tiles that show a Mexican peasant leaning against a cactus. I always think that's a wonderful icon and clearly that would be from somebody that's writing *about* the Southwest, not writing from the inside. Anybody here knows better than to lean against a cactus. I think that's a good example of somebody imposing a view, as opposed to somebody simply sharing a view. (171)

But more often the lament shows up in a harsher criticism of the ease with which we ignore, in Adrienne Rich's words, "the spirits / of place who understand travel but not amnesia" ("The Spirit of Place," Gelpi and Gelpi 99). Rich's criticism is similar to that expressed by Harjo of the "people in the towns and in the cities / learning not to hear the ground as it spun around / beneath them" (*SHSH* 18), and to Donald Hall's lament that "in America, the past exists / in the library. / It is not the wind on the stone" (30).

This amnesic placelessness sometimes affects non-Euro-Americans most keenly, as evidenced by the bitter satire in the lyric "moving camp too far" by Shoshoni-Chippewa poet nila northSun:

> i can't speak of
>   many moons
>   moving camp on travois
> i can't tell of
>   the last great battle
>   counting coup or
>   taking scalps
> i don't know what it
>   was to hunt buffalo
>   or do the ghost dance
> but
> i can see an eagle
>   almost extinct
>   on slurpee plastic cups
> i can travel to pow wows
>   in campers & winnebagos
> i can eat buffalo meat
>   at the tourist burger stand
> i can dance to indian music
>   rock-n-roll hey-a-hey-o
> i can
>   & unfortunately
>   i do (Hobson 380)

Here we see the effects of placelessness as northSun, achingly aware of traditions and culture sacrificed to commercialism and modernization, vividly renders that loss. Dispossessed of the ability to read natural signs like the movement of the moon, or to pursue wild buffalo across an empty plain, the poet is reduced to interacting with nonhuman nature only through its representation on 7-Eleven promotional advertisements and in rolling pre-packaged-meat stalls. No longer able to write their worlds "from the inside" (as Rios puts it), the poet and many of those around her are, in the words of Carol Lee Sanchez, "urban Indians / feasting out of context / multilayered collages / of who we used to be" (Hobson 249).

Scott Russell Sanders discusses this type of fierce nostalgia in his collection of essays *Staying Put*, defining the problem as a uniquely American one:

> The two Greek roots of *nostalgia* literally mean *return pain*. The pain comes not from returning home but from longing to return. Perhaps it is inevitable that a nation of immigrants—who shoved aside the native tribes of this continent, who enslaved and transported Africans, who still celebrate motion as if humans were dust motes—that such a nation would lose the deeper meaning of this word. A footloose people, we find it difficult to honor the lifelong, bone-deep attachment to place. We are slow to acknowledge the pain in yearning for one's native ground, the deep anguish in not being able, ever, to return. (14)

It is this reluctance to acknowledge "the pain in yearning for one's native ground, the deep anguish in not being able, ever, to return" that northSun, along with numerous other ecopoets, attempts to address. Wallace Stevens once wrote that "it would be enough / If we were ever, just once, at the middle, fixed / In This Beautiful World of Ours and not as now, // Helplessly at the edge" (430). The tragedy Sanders and northSun point to is not only that we now live "helplessly at the edge" of "This Beautiful World of Ours" rather than "at the middle, fixed," but also that our culture has almost completely lost the ability even to recognize the extent of our placelessness. As alien moderns, contemporary ecopoets consistently aim to create place-worlds that can help move us into an awareness not only of the interanimation that exists between ourselves and the rest of the world, but also of our own ignorance concerning our multifaceted need for it.

The more we overcome this ignorance, and the more we view the rest of our world as place and home, the more care we will take not to damage it. Carolyn Merchant explains that for centuries an organic view of the universe—one that viewed "the earth as a living organism and nurturing mother"—offered unquestioned cultural sanctions against damaging the natural world: "One does not readily slay a mother, dig into her entrails for gold, or mutilate her body. As long as the earth was conceptualized as alive and sensitive, it could be considered a breach of human ethical behavior to carry out destructive acts against it" (*RE* 43). While this organic worldview is no longer an option for most people living in the West, it is once again analogous to the perspective, offered by ecopoets, that insists we view the world as "place" rather than as "resources" to be used, or simply "the environment."[3] A place is much less likely to be abused than a mere geographical location to which we don't belong. As Hans Peter Duerr puts it, "People do not exploit a nature that speaks to them" (92).[4]

WHILE VIRTUALLY ALL ecopoets are indeed place-makers who repeatedly encourage us to value and create place, their writings simultaneously push readers to appreciate and even revere *space*. It is this concept that I think is most consistently overlooked in discussions, not only of ecopoets, but of nature writers in general. For while most critics readily consider place in nature writing, space is usually denigrated (as in Jerry Brown's statement) rather than valued.

This denigration is easy to understand, especially because we normally interpret space as the opposite of place and thus as placelessness. As Tuan explains,

> Spaciousness is closely associated with the sense of being free. Freedom implies space; it means having the power and enough room in which to act. Being free has several levels of meaning. Fundamental is the ability to transcend the present condition, and this transcendence is most simply manifest as the elementary power to move. (*SP* 52)

Based on this explanation, "spaciousness" would indeed appear to be a value that ecopoets would deemphasize and even criticize, arguing that the last thing we should do is attempt to transcend our present situation. For instance, in "Those Who Want Out," Levertov chastises would-be transcenders whose "vision / consumes them" while "they think all the time / of the city in space," by which she means, in this instance, literal outer space:

> they long for the permanent colony,
> not just a lab up there, the whole works,
> malls, racquet courts, hot tubs, state-of-the-art
> ski machines, entertainment . . . Imagine it, they think,
> way out there, outside of "nature," unhampered,
> a place contrived by man, supreme
> triumph of reason. They know it will happen,
> *They who do not love the earth.*
> (*The Life Around Us* 9, Levertov's ellipses and italics)

It is these people "who want out" to whom Berry repeatedly points in his efforts to convince us not to "think big," but to learn, instead, to "think little." To put it differently, ecopoets are rarely "exemptionalists" (the term is biologist E. O. Wilson's); they neither endorse nor believe in humans' ability to "exempt" themselves from their own biological futures so that they don't have to "go the way of the dinosaurs." [5]

Yet Tuan's explanation of spaciousness does not stop here, with the idea of transcendence; in fact, he argues that this supposed ability to "transcend the present condition" is actually fool's gold, in that the freedom associated with spaciousness only *appears* to offer the means to master the world beyond us. In truth, as we move into space, we discover, ironically, the extent of our limitations, rather than our freedom:

> When the Paleolithic hunter drops his hand ax and picks up a bow and arrow, he takes a step forward in overcoming space and yet space expands before him: things once beyond his physical reach and mental horizon now form a part of his world. Imagine a man of our time who learns first to ride a bicycle, then to drive a sports car, and eventually to pilot a small aircraft. He makes successive gains in speed; greater and greater distances are overcome. He conquers space but does not nullify its sensible size; on the contrary, space continues to open out for him. (*SP* 53)

Thus the more we move into space, the more we realize its vastness as it expands before us, helping us to understand our own smallness and producing an attitude of humility. As Thoreau put it, nature "invites us to lay our eye level with her smallest leaf, and take an insect view of its plain."

When applied to environmental issues, Tuan's discussion of space fits in nicely with what Levertov calls the "unknowing" of humanity (*TJL* 13). The simple fact is that despite our sometimes boundless faith in science and knowledge, we just don't know much about the places we inhabit, and the more we learn about the natural world (including humankind), the more we realize how much we do not, and probably cannot, know. The geneticist Richard Dawkins makes this point in poetic fashion in *Unweaving the Rainbow: Science, Delusion, and the Appetite for Wonder*, in which he discusses the human incapacity to comprehend our own genetic makeup: "We are digital archives of the African Pliocene, even of the Devonian seas; walking repositories of wisdom out of the old days. You could spend a lifetime reading in this ancient library and die unsated by the wonder of it" (289). This sense of epistemological limits echoes Emily Dickinson's ironic definition of nature as what we "have no art to say— / So impotent Our Wisdom is / To her simplicity."

Ultimately, then, while the process of place-making is a vital activity in the work of ecopoets, we should also realize that it is almost always balanced or, better yet, harmonized, with a healthy dose of *space-consciousness*, since to see oneself as a metaphorical place-maker is to be tempted also to see oneself as owner, or even literal creator, of the surrounding landscape. So in the world of ecopoetry, we hear Jeffers's advice to "remember that the life of mankind is like the life of a man, a flutter from darkness to darkness / Across the bright hair of a fire" (42). In this world the poet views him- or herself as one "longing to capture the horse with only one hair from its mane" and is grateful for the inability to grasp more (Bly *WHI* 19). As May Swenson puts it, "I hope they never get a rope on you, weather. I hope they never put a bit in your mouth" ("Weather" 66). Maxine Kumin expresses this notion well in her discussion of Mary Oliver, who Kumin says is constantly "reaching for the unattainable while grateful for its unattainability" (19). For poets, this awareness is important in that it "respects the immediacy and complexity of an evolving world that lies always just beyond the grasp of language" (Gilcrest 148).

Oliver's "Her Grave," an elegy for her recently buried dog, displays a keen awareness of what I am calling the "spatial" quality of the world. The poem begins with lines that, through the details they provide, relive the deep affection the speaker has felt for the dog. The speaker next introduces a series of questions asserting the absence of animal arrogance ("Does the hummingbird think he himself invented his crimson throat? Do the cranes crying out in the high clouds / think it is all their own music . . . ?") interspersed with statements concerning the relationship between dog and master; in doing so she renders two of the poem's main themes, humility and gratitude, both of which result from an appreciation of metaphoric space. After these questions and declarations, Oliver comes to her climactic response, a response both to the death and to its lessons: "Nor will I argue it, or pray for anything but modesty, and / not to be angry" (NASP 14–15). In this poem we observe an essential humility. Rather than regarding herself as somehow owner of the dog whose death she is mourning, she recognizes herself as receiver of a gift which, like the hummingbird's crimson throat and the cranes' music, is to be celebrated and relished rather than controlled or viewed with pride. When she voices the lines "A dog can never tell you what she knows from the / smells of the world, but you know, watching her, that you know / almost nothing," she demonstrates her awareness of and appreciation for the spaciousness of the world, of which she is nearly completely ignorant. She reasserts that humility in her supplication not to be angry, since anger would imply that she has lost something she owns and deserves to keep, rather than a gift.

Perhaps the best-known ecopoetic example of an appreciation of space and what Diane Bonds calls the "ownerlessness" of the world (13) comes in the closing lines of A. R. Ammons's "Corsons Inlet":

> I see narrow orders, limited tightness, but will
> not run to that easy victory:
>   still around the looser, wider forces work:
>   I will try
>   to fasten into order enlarging grasps of disorder, widening
>   scope, but enjoying the freedom that

Scope eludes my grasp, that there is no finality of vision,
that I have perceived nothing completely,
    that tomorrow a new walk is a new walk. (*SP* 46)

A recognition of the spaciousness of the world offers us the awareness that
the forms and order we notice in the natural world, while certainly pres-
ent, offer a too-easy victory. The poet's job is, indeed, "to fasten into order
enlarging grasps of disorder," but an ecopoetry will "enjoy the freedom"
that presents itself as we move into space, recognizing that with our limited
faculties of perception, "there is no finality of vision."[6] Emblematic of this
theme are the visible lines on the page that, instead of forming a uniform
block justified against the margin, resemble waves approaching the beach,
waves that proceed from a spaciousness still almost completely unknown
to humankind, that of the ocean. By pointing to this and other examples of
unattainable space, Ammons gratefully reminds us that "tomorrow a new
walk is a new walk."

ULTIMATELY, neither place nor space is sufficient alone; the two concepts
are interdependent and represent a "complex interplay . . . , the thrill of the
open road and the certainty of home, westering and dwelling, migration
and habitation, innovation and tradition, weav[ing] its way throughout our
collective and personal histories" (Franklin and Steiner 4). As Tuan puts it,

> Human lives are a dialectical movement between shelter and venture, at-
> tachment and freedom. In open space one can become intensely aware of
> place; and in the solitude of a sheltered place the vastness of space beyond
> acquires a haunting presence. A healthy being welcomes constraint and
> freedom, the boundedness of place and the exposure of space. (*SP* 54)

Throughout contemporary nature poetry runs this idea that a "healthy
being"—indeed, a healthy society—"welcomes constraint and freedom,
the boundedness of place and the exposure of space." As Berry has written,
"The wild and the domestic now often seem isolated values, estranged from
one another. And yet these are not exclusive polarities like good and evil.
There can be continuity between them, and there must be" (*LLH* 18).

Berry and other ecopoets insist that a sense of place ("domesticity") provides us not only with shelter and safety but also a desire to protect and "steward" the land and environment to which we belong. Such an ambition is part of a healthy ecological worldview that must also include a recognition of space ("wildness"), which teaches us the need for humility in an incomprehensible world that demands our caution in relation to it. "What we require, then," as Buell puts it, "is neither disparagement nor celebration of place-sense but an account of those specific conditions under which it significantly furthers what Relph calls environmental humility, an awakened place-awareness that is also mindful of its limitations and respectful that place molds us as well as vice versa" (253). Frost does declare, then, that a poem provides "a momentary stay against confusion" (and thus a way of making place), but he also reminds us that "something there is that doesn't love a wall." And Ammons follows the space-conscious line "I know nothing" with a place-making one: "Still, I cannot help singing." To comprehend the place-spaciousness of nature is to be able to say, with Roethke, "All finite things reveal infinitude" ("The Far Field" 195).

Some poets tend to emphasize one side of the binary over the other. Stevens, for example, stresses space-consciousness over place-making, writing that "we live in a place / That is not our own and, much more, not ourselves" (383), and that those who "go crying / The world is myself, life is myself, / Breathing as if they breathed themselves," are "full of their ugly lord" (361). Others are much more intent on place-making, as I discussed above. But regardless of how the actual ratio of place to space breaks down, the two forces work together: attention to the finitude of place synchronizes with the boundlessness of space. In fact, Edward J. Brunner goes so far as to say that this harmonization of place and space is actually the location where poetry takes place. In discussing Merwin, Brunner writes that poetry is "the problematic area that breaks into existence when the poet once again realizes these two worlds [the one humans create and its chaotic, unmanageable opposite] as they intersect, overlie, and disrupt each other" (287). In other words, poetry happens, to paraphrase Brunner, where place meets space. Whether this definition can be applied to all poetry or not is debatable (Brunner applies it only to Merwin), but in ecopoetry the characterization almost always applies.

THIS INTERACTION between place and space within ecopoetry further elucidates the three primary characteristics I earlier suggested for the mode. Paying close attention to the places in which they reside leads the poets to an increased awareness of the ecological interconnection between all the inhabiters of that particular place. And a healthy space-consciousness is closely connected to the other primary characteristics, since such a perspective is inherently humble and by definition brings to light the inadequacies in human attempts to control, master, or even fully understand the world around them.

Ecopoets deemphasize the individual ego by making place, by offering readers an opportunity to view themselves as members of what David Abram calls a "more-than-human world," while simultaneously maintaining that that world will always elude our attempts to contain or grasp it, either literally or figuratively. Often, the means to achieving place- and space-consciousness is an immersion of the self in the natural community, not by leaving the ego behind or by becoming a transparent eyeball, but by recognizing that we are members and citizens of (in Aldo Leopold's phrase) a "land-community" to which we belong but will never master or fully comprehend (204).

CHAPTER TWO

Divided against Ourselves

Wendell Berry

The only hope then lies not in identification with either pole of opposition, but in discovering a more inclusive, sustaining reality—some larger grammar in which the words *culture* and *wilderness* may both be spoken.

—John Elder, *Imagining the Earth*

WENDELL BERRY is one of a long line of thinkers attempting to overcome (or at least respond to) the modern split between human and nonhuman nature. Throughout his work Berry has addressed modern alienation by opposing the setting of culture and nature at odds, and by arguing for the importance of understanding the interrelation and interdependence between the human and nonhuman worlds. By applying Tuan's place-space framework to Berry's poetics, we can more easily comprehend Berry's response to this modern dilemma. In his place- and space-conscious poetry, which emerges from his Kentucky farming background and Protestant heritage, Berry stresses the need for people to recover an active, physical, sustainable relationship with the landscape around them and thereby discover the extent to which we both depend on, and ultimately fail to comprehend, the transhuman world. Berry's work, with its focus on the interaction between the domestic and the wild, offers a keen sense of place- and space-consciousness that repeatedly emphasizes the extent to which we are both connected to and essentially ignorant of wild nature.

In addition to offering a theory and vocabulary with which to analyze Berry's poetry, the place-space framework also provides tools that allow us to evaluate and criticize Berry's response to this modern rift. For instance, an examination of the terminology Berry occasionally uses in his essays—specifically, oppositional terms like "culture" and "nature," "domesticity" and "wildness"—reveals that despite his obvious commitment to attitudes I am calling place- and space-consciousness, his vocabulary at times threatens to undermine the very project he undertakes in his poetry; in many ways it reinforces the dualism he strives to overcome. This terminology lacks the ability to communicate concisely and adequately the concepts and values Berry wants to convey in his work. Consequently, a need exists for a vocabulary capable of succinctly describing the attitudes Berry and other ecopoets want to articulate. Tuan's place-space framework offers just such a vocabulary.

BEFORE TURNING TO my analysis of Berry's use of the limiting civilization/wilderness vocabulary, I want to look at some central themes appearing in his poetry and use them to further elucidate the Tuanian place-space synergism. There is little question that Wendell Berry is a place-maker as I defined it in chapter 1; that is, he attempts to move his audience out of an existence in an abstract space where we are simply visitors in an unknown neighborhood and into a recognition of our present surroundings as place and thus as home. Critics have extensively discussed this aspect of Berry's writing, most prominently with regard to his prose. Scott Russell Sanders, for instance, compares Berry's fiction to that of writers like Hardy, in whose novels "landscape is no mere scenery, no flimsy stage set, but rather the energizing *medium* from which human lives emerge and by which those lives are bounded and measured" ("Speaking" 183). Sanders contrasts Berry to another Kentucky author, Bobbie Ann Mason, in whose fiction "nature supplies an occasional metaphor to illustrate a character's dilemma—a tulip tree cut down when it was about to bloom, a rabbit with crushed legs on the highway—exactly as K-Mart or Cat Chow or the Phil Donahue Show supply analogues" (191). For Berry, on the other hand, "no matter how much the land has been neglected or abused, no matter how ignorant of their environment people may have become, nature is the medium in which life transpires, and its prime source of values and meaning and purpose" (191). Scott Slovic makes a similar point regarding Berry's essays, noting that "Berry manages to suggest that both the language and the ideas of his essay originate somehow in the natural place and in his family's long association with the place rather than in his own mind. Rather than making the land part of him, he and his essay grow out of the land" (127–128).

The same goes for Berry's verse, in which he aims for the type of poetry Thoreau said "is nothing but healthy speech." Berry comments on this definition, interpreting it to mean "speech that is not only healthy in itself, but conducive to the health of the speaker, giving him a true and vigorous relation to the world" (*CH* 14). This concept of "a true and vigorous relation to the world" is crucial to Berry's poetry, for he holds that "nothing can be its own context. Meaning and value are not generated by parts, but are conferred by the whole" (*SBW* 167). Thus, "when we include ourselves as parts or belongings of the world we are trying to preserve, then obviously we can no longer think of the world as 'the environment'—something out there around us. We can see that our relation to the world surpasses mere connection and verges on identity" (*ATC* 74–75). To recognize our relationship to nature as one verging on identity is to feel "in place," and probably more than any other concept, Berry's poetry is about this notion. The poems' themes, their driving motivation, even their formal aspects, with their orderly lines and consistent lengths, all reinforce the place-filled nature of Berry's verse.

A good example of Berry's connection to his place can be found in early poems like "The Strangers," about travelers who stop to ask directions of the speaker: "Where are we? Where / does this road go?" The speaker explains to the readers that these strangers have lost a connection to the land and are consequently unable to see the places they visit, knowing only the names on the map. In attempting to direct the travelers, the speaker finds himself at a loss, since his knowledge is based on an intimate relationship with the land, six generations in the making, and they are unfamiliar with the place, not "conversant with its trees / and stones." The poem concludes with the strangers waiting for an answer that the speaker says he knows "too well to speak," and he compares himself to "an Indian / before the alien ships" (*CM* 37).

This 1973 poem conveys a concept that Berry's work returns to again and again: that it is possible to know a place well, and that this knowledge may separate a person from those who choose not to know that place. Notice also the theme that numerous ecopoets take up, the inadequacy of language. The speaker associates himself with precolonial American Indians, comparing his place-knowledge to theirs and implying, hyperbolically, that the language barrier between himself and the strangers is similar to the one between Native people and the "alien" Europeans. He hasn't the linguistic means to articulate the knowledge acquired through years of living in and with his place.

Berry also works with this idea in his poem "The Record," from *Entries* (1994), in which a "young friend" asks the speaker to record the voice of an "old friend" who has gathered a lifetime of knowledge of Cane Run, his place. The youth explains that that knowledge "is precious" and "should be saved." The speaker's response is sympathetic—"I know the panic of that wish to save / the vital knowledge of the old times, handed down"—but he also admonishes the young friend for believing in a royal road to place-knowledge. He tells him to "stay and listen" until he or the old man dies, to "live here / as one who knows these things," and to tell his children and tell them to tell their children. By doing so, the young man can emulate the creek, which "steps downward / over the rocks, saying the same changing thing / in the same place as it goes" (*E* 9–10). As in "The Strangers," in this poem we see the affirmation that place matters, and that its experience and appreciation transcend our ability to communicate it or to save it in some simple way. The way to know (and save) place is to live it, and to live it fully.

One of Berry's favorite (and most-discussed) place-making metaphors, therefore, is marriage. In his poems matrimony refers to a lifelong commitment not only to another person but to the land, the connector of all things past, present, and future. Marriage for Berry is an analogue for a person's devotion to his or her place and all that comes with it.[1] In "The Current," for example, Berry renders a profound bond with the land, a sustainable relationship that also connects him to the past and to people who have come before him, as well as to those who follow; for having "married" the ground, he is now the "descendent" of the "old tribespeople" who preceded him, and he is also related, through the land, to "the bearers of his own blood" who will follow him and work the farm (*CP* 119). The current in the poem's title refers to a metaphorical river flowing from past to future, with the man in the poem representing the current's present-moment existence. The poem also asserts that what takes place now, that which is *current*, is not isolated from what has come before or will appear in the future. For Berry, as Bernard Quetchenbach has said, "the past and future are palpable through the reenactment of lives and the embodiment of ideas and lifeways in succeeding generations" (127).

Another way Berry attempts to make place is by constantly reminding his readers that, ultimately, we are all literally and biologically connected to everything else, for we all die and our bodies nourish the rest of nature. In "Enriching the Earth," the speaker, presumably a farmer, says that

> to serve the earth,
> not knowing what I serve, gives a wideness
> and a delight to the air, ...
> [. . . . .]

After death, willing or not, the body serves,
entering the earth. And so what was heaviest
and most mute is at last raised up into song. (*CP* 110)

Similarly, in "The Farmer among the Tombs," the farmer says that he is "op-
pressed by all the room taken up by the dead"; he therefore declares, "Plow
up the graveyards! Haul off the monuments!" so that the dead may "nour-
ish their graves / and go free" (*CP* 105). Berry has written, "We thus come
again to the paradox that one can become whole only by the responsible
acceptance of one's partiality" (*UA* 123). John Elder, commenting on this
statement, writes, "To be partial is the opposite of inertness, in the chemical
sense of that term: an element that will not enter into combination. Partial-
ness, living rooted in one's own perpetual decay, allows for connection, for
the cross-pollination that lets flowers bear their message from the earth"
(60–61).

A poem that connects the marriage theme with this celebration of death
is "The Clear Days," where Berry writes that "until the heart has found /
Its native piece of ground // The day withholds its light, / the eye must stay
unlit. // The ground's the body's bride, / who will not be denied" (*CP* 165).
Here the poet makes explicit the eternal commitment between the land
and the body. The point, as expressed by Leonard Scigaj, is that "we are
intimately connected to the soil—not just dependent on it for food, but as
organic plants ourselves, growing and decaying" (172). And obviously, this
insight is cause for delight rather than regret for Berry, who prays elsewhere
that his life might be "a patient willing descent into the grass" ("The Wish
to Be Generous," *CP* 114).

One poem that expresses well Berry's devotion to the relationship be-
tween humans and the land is "Where," a long poem from *Clearing* (1977)
that Berry extensively revised and condensed for his 1984 *Collected Poems.*
This poem narrates the passage of Lane's Landing, the fifty-acre farm Berry
and his family purchased in the late 1960s, from wilderness to productive
farm to the scarred and "ruined" land that he now owns and works. After
describing the fecundity of the land before it was bought by one who ne-
glected it (because of his "mind cast loose / in whim and greed"), the poet

renders the tragedy of that loss, that its abundance did not last as it might have, "given / a live, husbandly tradition," but was instead "ruined" by "one lifetime of our history" (*CP* 178). As Andrew Angyal says of this poem, "Berry presents the history of his farm as a parable of the American frontier and an indictment of the reckless habits that quickly exhausted the land's natural richness and abundance. 'Where' is both a personal credo and a contemporary ecological statement of the need to change both land management practices and cultural attitudes toward the land" (126). As Berry puts it elsewhere, "The mistakes of old // become the terrors of the young" ("Handing Down," *CP* 38).

"Where" is reminiscent of an episode extolling the virtue of work in Berry's verse play "The Bringer of Water" from *Farming: A Handbook* (1970). In this scene Nathan Coulter has met his fiancé, Hannah Feltner, to show her the rundown farm he has just bought. In explaining why he was willing to take on the challenge of restoring the overused land, Nathan speaks out of a conviction related to Berry's theme in "Where":

> A lifetime won't be enough
> to bring it back. A man
> would have to live maybe
> five hundred years
> to make it good again
> — or learn something of the cost
> of not making it good.
> But hard as it is, I accept
> this fate. I even like it
> a little — the idea of making
> my lifetime one of the several
> it will take to bring back
> the possibilities of this place
> that used to be here. (*FH* 91–93)

The fate Nathan speaks of has to do with working this particular farm, this particular place. He must devote his life to caring for and understanding this specific plot of land. Again, we see the land marrying both its current inhabiters and those in the past. (As Berry says in "Rising," the good farmer's life "does not travel / along any road, toward / any other place, / but is a journey back and forth / in rows" [CP 242].)

But in this case the relationship is based not only on a devotion to the land but also on a mournful recognition of its defilement. As Elder explains, "To perceive in the contemporary abuse of natural cycles the end of processes on which our life has depended is also to experience the precious wholeness at every point of the process, beginning and end alike" (58). Berry's poems thus challenge and encourage their readers to view "the precious wholeness" around them as a place, and as their fate. For "to love a chosen place truly," as Elder paraphrases Berry, "is to learn that earth and mankind are one" (53). This does not mean that everyone must become a farmer but rather that all of us should view the world in a way that "verges on identity" and enjoys "the idea of making / my lifetime one of the several / it will take to bring back / the possibilities of this place / that used to be here." Farming, in Berry's work, serves as both a literal subject for his poems and a metaphor and model for place-making of all kinds. For him, farming means remaining in one place long enough to know and care for it well. It means, in Tuanian parlance, making place.

ALONG WITH THIS place-consciousness comes a keen appreciation for the wilder aspects of the natural world; throughout his writings Berry asserts the fundamental human need for interacting with the wildness Thoreau claimed was necessary for the preservation of the world. This appreciation of wildness leads to an acute space-consciousness that harmonizes with and counterbalances Berry's place-centeredness. Just as the farm takes on both literal and figurative connotations for Berry as he attempts to demonstrate its role in making place, so wildness represents the actual wilderness beyond human domestication, as well as a more metaphorical wilderness that presupposes elements of the world that remain beyond our ability to know them.

One of the primary roots of many of our ecological and epistemological problems, according to Berry, is that we lack "the humbling awareness of the insufficiency of knowledge, of mystery" (SBW 50). Therefore, we must preserve wilderness because "we need it. We need wilderness of all kinds, large and small, public and private. We need to go now and again into places where our work is disallowed, where our hopes and plans have no standing" (*HE* 146). Berry essentially argues that we all too often fail to comprehend just how much we do not know. "The system of systems is enclosed within mystery," he writes, "in which some truth can be known, but never all truth" (*SBW* 49). Regardless of our continuing acquisition of "facts," implies Berry, when it comes to the fundamental workings of the world, we are practically illiterate.

Encountering the ultimate unknowability of the wildness beyond civilization has the power to lead us to a healthy realization of our own insignificance in the world. As Berry explains in his essay "A Native Hill," to understand one is to know the other; to realize the world's mystery is to recognize our own smallness:

> To walk in the woods, mindful only of the *physical* extent of it, is to go perhaps as owner, or as knower, confident of one's own history and of one's own importance. But to go there, mindful as well of its temporal extent, of the age of it, and of all that led up to the present life of it, and of all that will probably follow it, is to feel oneself a flea in the pelt of a great living thing, the discrepancy between its life and one's own so great that it cannot be imagined. One has come into the presence of mystery. (*LLH* 204–205)

This unknowable mystery is what leads us to notice our "flealike" quality in the grand scheme of the universe which, as Berry puts it in one of his Sabbath poems, is constantly "outreaching understanding" (*S* 7).

Berry continues this thought later in the same essay, when he argues that we must "understand what the land is":

> And to come to that understanding it is necessary, even now, to leave the regions of our conquest — the cleared fields, the towns and cities, the highways — and re-enter the woods. For only there can a man encounter the silence and the darkness of his own absence. Only in this silence and darkness can he recover the sense of the world's longevity, of its ability to thrive without him, of his inferiority to it and his dependence on it.

Perhaps then, having heard that silence and seen that darkness, he will grow humble before the place and begin to take it in—to learn *from it* what it is. (*LLH* 207)

Notice here that this awareness of space, of the world's wildness that is beyond human knowledge, leads not to alienation for Berry, but to relationship, for once he internalizes "his inferiority to it and his dependence on" the land, "he may come into its presence as he never has before, and he will arrive in his place and want to remain. His life will grow out of the ground like the other lives of the place, and take its place among them" (*LLH* 207). The same idea appears in his Sabbath poem "The Intellect So Ravenous to Know," where Berry renders "an old field worn out by disease // of human understanding" and encourages us to realize that we exist within an "order we are ignorant of" (*S* 35–36).

This insight, that a cognizance of our own insignificance leads to an awareness of relationship with the transhuman world, appears throughout Berry's poetry and is usually related to what he calls our "obligation of care." Instead of viewing nature "as a machine or as the sum of its known, separable, and decipherable parts," Berry insists on our responsibility to care for the world around us, asserting that doing so prevents us from imposing our own will, based on our own limited knowledge, on the natural world. For "care allows creatures to escape our explanations into their actual presence and their essential mystery. In taking care of fellow creatures, we acknowledge that they are not ours; we acknowledge that they belong to an order and a harmony of which we ourselves are parts" ("OC"). Thus Berry presents poems like his well-known "To the Unseeable Animal," addressed to an unknown creature who is a manifestation of the world's beauty and mystery. He tells the animal, "That we do not know you / is your perfection / and our hope. The darkness / keeps us near you" (*CP* 140–141). The darkness of the wild, the fact that "we do not know" it, is what keeps us close to the nonhuman world that surrounds us.

Berry therefore revels in his ignorance and insignificance. He says, along with his Mad Farmer (a jeremiadic persona the poet often adopts), "Give your approval to all you cannot / understand. Praise ignorance, for what man / has not encountered he has not destroyed" ("Manifesto: The Mad

Farmer Liberation Front," *CP* 151). Humility is the chief reason for maintaining awareness of the mystery of the wild. For "to be divided against nature, against wildness, . . . is a human disaster, because it is to be divided against ourselves. It confines our identity as creatures entirely within the bounds of our own understanding, which is invariably a mistake because it is invariably reductive. It reduces our largeness, our mystery, to a petty and sickly comprehensibility" (*HE* 141). This humility contrasts sharply with the mindset that, as Berry quotes Gurney Norman, "believes there *is* no context until *it* gets there" (*SBW* 115). Quetchenbach makes this point regarding the relationship between culture and wilderness:

> Berry is as aware as any contemporary poet of the importance of culture in forming the individual. He tends to see the "wild" as anything that exists outside of the domestic order tentatively, and often locally, established and maintained by culture. Culture can be seen as both a necessary protection from the unknown wilderness and a way to translate that wilderness into understandable terms. In either case, the possibility of a deep intuitive connection between wilderness and the human unconscious is at least sharply qualified by the inaccessibility or fundamental mysteriousness of that connection. (132)

To be humble, for Berry, is to understand and accept this "inaccessibility or fundamental mysteriousness," along with our own unimportance; in that unimportance lies our relationship to the more-than-human world.

THUS THE place-space paradigm offers a tool by which to analyze Berry's poetry, and a vocabulary with which to discuss the philosophy underlying his poetics. Through this Tuanian lens we see that Berry's response to the human-nature split is a call to connect with literal, local, physical places. He also demonstrates a highly developed sense of space in his point that a true and vital connection to the land reveals the extent to which we are incapable of fully knowing those places. This type of analysis can be performed on any number of ecopoets (as we will see in the following chapters), helping us better understand their work and their response to the modern rupture between human and nonhuman nature.

Analysis, however, is not the only function the place-space framework offers; the theory also serves as a valuable tool with which to assess the assumptions underlying a writer's poetics and rhetoric. For instance, when we use the framework to examine Berry's response to the split between humans and the rest of the natural world, we discover an inconsistency in the vocabulary he often employs. For while his poetry exhibits a place- and space-conscious perspective on the world, the vocabulary he chooses to express that awareness at times defeats his ultimate purpose.

In order to understand this point, a brief explanation of the linguistic problem is necessary. The English language has always betrayed a confusion concerning the boundary between the human and nonhuman worlds. Linguistically, the either/or construction of the question—human or nonhuman—is a faulty one. Our language demonstrates that rather than being either human *or* natural, we are both human *and* natural, both civilized *and* wild.

For example, "animal," in its earliest usage (1330, according to the *Middle English Dictionary* [MED]; 1398, according to the *Oxford English Dictionary* [OED]), referred simply to "a living creature," or more properly, "anything living" (OED), including human beings. It comes from the Latin *animale*, neuter of *animalis*, meaning simply "having the breath of life" (Weekley). Additionally, *animalis* is derived from *anima*—life—which is related to *animus* —mind, spirit, soul (Barnhart).

We can draw a couple of important conclusions from this evidence. First, in its earliest English appearance, "animal" made no distinction between human and nonhuman; humans were a subset of animals. Working in the other direction, we see also the spiritual and psychological foundations of our modern conception of "animal," which contains within its root (*animus*) the implication that both animal and human are characterized by mind and spirit.

Likewise, the Middle English word "beste" (OED 1220, MED 1330), from the Old French *beste*, from vulgar Latin *besta*, and from Latin *bestia*, "wild animal," did not describe nonhumans exclusively. According to the OED, the word "in early times explicitly includ[ed] man," as when Chaucer writes, "Asketh not me, quod I, whether man be a reasonable beest mortal" (*Boethius* I. vi. 27). Thus the need existed early on to distinguish between "beste doumb and louer" and a "resounable, two-foted beste" (Kuhn). Even in their earliest manifestations, our words for describing the natural world included both human and nonhuman nature.

This confusion exists today as well. Despite the fact that we normally view ourselves as separate from and above the natural, carnal, and mortal world of the animals, minerals, and vegetables, most of us maintain some sort of intuitive, experiential conviction that we are indeed embedded within and members of that world. Scientific evidence for this claim has been spelled out in studies that demonstrate, for example, the "human" qualities (sociability, intelligence, communication, technology) of primates, dolphins, dogs, and other animals. In addition, according to the biologist E. O. Wilson, "biophilia" — "the urge to affiliate with other forms of life" — is a part of who we are, and is therefore evidence of our own naturalness (85). "We are," argues Wilson, "a biological species [that] will find little ultimate meaning apart from the remainder of life" (112). David Orr explains, "Biophilia is inscribed in the brain itself, expressing tens of thousands of years of evolutionary experience" (138). As Frederick Turner puts it, "Our bodies and brains are a result of evolution, which is a natural process so paradigmatic that it could almost be said to be synonymous with nature itself" ("Cultivating" 42). Thus, just as we sometimes assert that we are somehow separate and apart from nature, we simultaneously maintain confidence in some sort of bond we share with the rest of the natural world. What these contradictory notions represent for us is an ambivalence regarding where (and whether) to draw the human/nonhuman boundary.

No wonder, then, that divisive binaries based on terms like "civilization" and "wilderness" prove insufficient when discussing human-nonhuman relationships. As numerous critics have pointed out, our inherited civilization-wilderness terminology is highly problematic and fraught with potential pitfalls.[2] The main problem with separating wildness from civilization is that doing so implies a definite if not clearly demarcated line between the two states of existence, a line that in many important ways is fictional. As Max Oelschlaeger puts it, "Our prevailing definitions of 'wildness' and 'wilderness' preclude recognition of nature as a spontaneous and naturally organized system in which all parts are harmoniously interrelated" (Idea 8). Instead, we assume that civilization cannot be wild, and that the wild cannot

be civilized. This damaging and inconsistent separation threatens to discon-
nect humans from anything wild, anything beyond our control, including
nonhuman nature as well as those parts and functions of our own bodies we
do not understand. It is also developmentally damaging both to individu-
als and to the species, for as numerous studies conclude, there seems to be
a vital relationship between healthy human development and socialization
into a wild and natural environment.[3]

Frederick Turner discusses other negative results of "this ideological op-
position of culture and nature—with no mediating term," asserting that the
separation "has had real consequences" not only in terms of how we view
ourselves but also how we view the natural world: "More often than need
be, Americans confronted with a natural landscape have either exploited
it or designated it a wilderness area. The polluter and the ecology freak are
two faces of the same coin; they both perpetuate a theory about nature that
allows no alternative to raping it or tying it up in a plastic bag to protect
it from contamination" ("Cultivating" 45). Put simply, in our designation
of "nature" as that which is not human, we forgo our chances at an honest
and meaningful interaction with the natural world. Furthermore, within
the implication that civilization and wilderness oppose one another lies an
assumption that nothing "cultural" or "social" takes place within the wild,
when we know of course that animals form social groups, make homes, use
tools, and communicate with one another.

Oelschlaeger suggests an alternative perspective on our interaction with
the wild, one in which "wild nature and culture are understood as organi-
cally related." "Human beings are not pure thinking things ensconced within
Euroculture," he argues, "but beings whose thoughts and feelings are embod-
ied, centered, in an organic human nature fashioned in the web of life over
the longueurs of space and time, internally related to nature" (8–9). Yet while
Oelschlaeger's alternative certainly sounds compelling, understanding "wild
nature and culture as organically related" is a difficult intellectual move for
many of us to make, in that the two forces seem to be at such odds. Our very
terminology, the language itself, is implicated in the dilemma, for "wild," by
definition, means uncivilized, just as "civilized" means that culture has been
imposed on nature.[4] Clearly, then, achieving a consistent and convincing per-
spective on how we might healthfully interact with the more-than-human

world around us is going to be difficult as long as we rely on the terminology presently available to us. We need new terms.

The place-space framework offers an alternative vocabulary, one that allows us to discuss this interaction without reinforcing the separation, thus avoiding the pitfalls of the civilization/wilderness dichotomy. It is a revisioning of our relationship with the world, one that supplants the us/it dichotomy and replaces it with a perspective that views life as more of a continuum, made up not of two opposites (or even two sides of a coin) but of a wide variety of experiences and interactions. Some of these help us feel at home, as though we know our world, and some help us see that we do not, and in many ways cannot, feel like anything more than visitors in that world.

The principal difficulty for the inherited civilization/wilderness binary lies in attempting to describe or explain "the wild" at all, for the very phrase means something beyond our knowledge, something we cannot ever truly characterize or comprehend. We can ponder place, discuss the domestic, for we have experienced it directly and intimately. When it comes to the wilderness, though, mystery reigns. The place-space framework takes a different approach by exploring, not the actual phenomena of civilization and wildness, but the *human relationship* with both places we can know and those we are largely forbidden from understanding. The focus thus becomes the way humans interact with the domestic and with the wild. The place-space vocabulary comes much closer to describing what most ecopoets are doing: rendering their own experiences with the world.

BERRY IS CERTAINLY aware of the linguistic limitations of concepts like "civilization" and "wilderness":

> It is a mistake to proceed on the basis of an assumed division between nature and humanity, or wildness and domesticity. But it is also a mistake to assume that there is no difference between the natural and the human. If these things could be divided, our life would be far simpler and easier than it is, just as it would be if they were not different. Our problem, exactly, is that the human and the natural are indivisible, and yet are different. (*HE* 139)

In Berry's view, we make a mistake when we reduce the relationship in either direction, by backgrounding either the differences or the similarities. The complexity of the relationship between human and nature should not be overlooked: to separate civilization from wildness, and culture from nature, as if each term signifies a clearly defined component of the human-nature relationship, is to misunderstand the relationship completely. At another point Berry argues that "the dualism of domestic and wild certainly involves opposition and tension, but from the domestic point of view it also involves dependence; domestic structures that shut out, ignore, or destroy their wild sources are therefore doomed" (SBW 179). Civilization cannot exist without the wild, Berry maintains, for the two concepts are linked and interdependent.[5]

Accordingly, one of the primary projects of Berry's writings is to overcome this distinction by spotlighting the interdependence between nature and culture, between civilization and the wild. Often, he is successful, and the result is a poetry deeply rooted in place-space synergy. Yet at times, especially in his essays, his language becomes so invested in the very dichotomies he intends to surmount that he ends up reinforcing the dualism that separates people from the rest of nature. It is of note that this dualism is rare in his poetry; the problem for the most part is restricted to his prose. It is as if he is able to *render* an experience in such a way as to be consistent with his worldview, but he is less successful at *discussing* that experience without falling prey to these linguistic difficulties.

Consider, first, some of Berry's successful efforts at communicating the interaction between place- and space-conscious values. His vision is based on two different concepts of place: our literal, geographical place in the world; and our place in the cosmic sense, in terms of where we "belong" in what he calls an "updated, ecological version of the Great Chain of Being" (SBW 46–47).[6] In other words, one concept of place has to do with knowing the actual people and land around us; the other works from an implicit understanding of our own limits and essential ignorance. These two types of place neatly correspond to Tuan's place and space, and Berry holds that they "can be understood as explaining the difference and the division between good and evil. If we understand this concept of place carefully and fully enough, we can say simply that to be in place is good and to be out of place is evil, for where we are with respect to our place both in the order of things and on earth is the definition of our whereabouts with respect to God and our fellow creatures" (178). All of this is part of what Berry describes as an "ecological intelligence: a sense of the impossibility of acting or living alone or solely in one's own behalf, and this rests in turn upon a sense of the order upon which any life depends and of the proprieties of place within that order" (*SBW* 111). These "proprieties of place" proceed from an awareness of our connectedness to the world around us and from our realization that we exist within an established order we can never fully understand.

This interrelation appears throughout Berry's poetry, where place and space repeatedly lead into and out of each other. In the title poem of "The Country of Marriage," Berry writes, "You are the known way leading always to the unknown, / and you are the known place to which the unknown is always / leading me back" (*CP* 147). A similar theme appears in "The Stones," where Berry again uses eros as an analogy for his matrimonial devotion to the land. In this poem the farmer, having cleared a portion of land, learns from the rocks "the weariness that loves the ground." He responds to this insight with the line, "I must prepare a fitting silence" (*CP* 104). This silence is closely akin to space-consciousness, an attitude that consistently brings one back to place, to belonging. "On the Hill Late at Night" also interweaves place and space:

> The ripe grassheads bend in the starlight
> in the soft wind, beneath them the darkness
> of the grass, fathomless, the long blades
> rising out of the well of time. Cars
> travel the valley roads below me, their lights
> finding the dark, and racing on. Above
> their roar is a silence I have suddenly heard,
> and felt the country turn under the stars
> toward dawn. I am wholly willing to be here
> between the bright silent thousands of stars
> and the life of the grass pouring out of the ground.
> The hill has grown to me like a foot.
> Until I lift the earth I cannot move. (*CP* 113)

Notice here the poet's space-consciousness in his admission of his own essential ignorance, and how this attitude leads him to a bodily connection with the earth. The "fathomless[ness]" and "darkness" of the grass; the "silence" of the sky; the mystery of "the bright silent thousands of stars" and "the grass pouring out of the ground": all of these bring the speaker to a moment of utter connectedness, in which he feels organically affixed to the earth.

A similar theme guides "The Silence," which begins with a place-making question—"What must a man do to be at home in the world?"—then moves to its answer, a space-conscious one that asserts that one must learn to be "here / as though absent"; to go "beyond words into the woven shadows" of the world and "beyond / the sense of the weariness of engines and of [one's] own heart"; to hear "the silence / of the tongues of the dead tribesmen" who inhabited the land generations ago. To participate in these actions, the poem declares, is to appreciate the wildness and mystery of the world. And having prepared such an attitude within oneself, a person is then capable of seeing the wonder of the world and feeling a part of it, of making place in it and knowing what she or he must do "to be at home in the world."

Thus in Berry's work we often see a fundamental intermingling of place and space that avoids falling into the civilization/wilderness trap. In poems like these, he displays a proficiency for communicating his commitment to the interaction between his own place- and space-consciousness. He calls for a "landscape criticism," proposing "that humans should learn to behave properly with respect to nature so as to place their domestic economy harmoniously upon and within the sustaining and surrounding wilderness" (*HE* 151). The call is for an "essential double awareness of the physical presence of the natural world and of the immanence of mystery or divinity in the physical presence" (*CH* 17), and it advises that "one should rejoice in understanding, but rejoice also in failing to understand, for in that failure the mind is set free" (*CH* 32). Wildness in Berry's sense "becomes less a term indicating chaos, disorder, or threat than one suggesting a deeper coherence and harmony, as human culture and institutions are brought into closer alignment with the natural world" (Robinson 21).[7]

As I argued in chapter 1, ecopoets typically stress this nonadversarial and interdependent relationship between place and space, and Berry is certainly no different. Yet while the place-making and space-conscious *attitudes* he describes do not mutually exclude each other, his terms "civilization" and "wilderness" often do. For example, in the previously quoted lines from his 1983 essay "Poetry and Place," Berry focuses on the place-space relationship, relying on the words "domestic" and "wild." This passage highlights the difficulty of using such terms to explore the human-nature border:

> The dualism of domestic and wild certainly involves opposition and tension, but from the domestic point of view it also involves dependence; domestic structures that shut out, ignore, or destroy their wild sources are therefore doomed.

The passage begins in perfect consistency with the place-space framework: from the human point of view, we cannot "shut out, ignore, or destroy" the parts of the world we do not understand, without paying serious consequences. But in the following sentences, the linguistic limitations appear:

> Likewise, any wildness within human power that is not allowed for and sanctioned by domestic structures is therefore doomed. The ideal, as poets from Homer to Pound have instructed us, is harmony: the domestic must be placed within the wild—for the wild must always be larger—with such studied and elegant propriety as to preserve *both*. (*SBW* 179)

Notice that Berry calls for the use of domestic structures to "allow for" and "sanction" the wild, placing the domestic within the larger wildness. The problem of the idea of "the wild" is that it is "un-sanctioned" by the domestic; it cannot be "allowed for," or it is no longer wild.

My intent is not to quibble with Berry's argument per se, for I think he is exactly right. Practically speaking, if we are to maintain some of what he is calling "wildness" in our world, we must allow for it, sanction it, make a place for it, and preserve it. Berry's argument is right; it is the words we conventionally employ that are limiting. For what Berry presumably means here by "the wild" differs from what he describes numerous times elsewhere, namely a wildness that is also a part of the human world and should not be viewed as separate from it.[8] This point involves a subtle but important distinction, for the passage's current phrasing, encouraging a sanctioning of the wild by the domestic, is much different from the less dualistic language

I examined earlier, where Berry points out the perils involved in destroying places that help us maintain an awareness of our own limitations. Berry's point in this passage seems to be that we must maintain an appreciation for the parts of the world beyond our knowledge and control, as well as a recognition of our relation to and dependence on those parts of the world.

As it stands, however, the terminology in the passage undermines Berry's vision in two specific ways: it advocates assuming control over that which would cease to be itself were we to assume that control, and it presents the domestic and the wild as two distinguishable, if not separate, entities. As I demonstrated earlier, Berry is often able to communicate his vision by avoiding this imprecise and oppositional vocabulary; yet here, in drawing the sharp distinction between domestic and wild, his own terminology proves self-defeating. His passion, combined with his sincerity and powerful rhetoric, comes close to conveying the values and concepts he wants to communicate; yet having been built on a shaky foundation of an inconsistent vocabulary, the argument itself is marred.

Another example appears in Berry's 1985 "Preserving Wilderness," an essay that summarizes his argument for not dividing nature from culture. Berry again asserts the "indivisibility" of wildness and domesticity and criticizes both sides of a polarized environmental debate between wilderness preservation and industrial development; he contends that the controversy blurs the issue of the fundamental interrelationship between humans and nonhumans. Achieving a complementary accord between civilization and wilderness, culture and nature, claims Berry, is "the forever unfinished lifework of our species" (*HE* 139). Yet within this argument Berry repeatedly returns to the old terminology and thus again linguistically counters his message, as in his famous line, "The only thing we have to preserve nature with is culture; the only thing we have to preserve wildness with is domesticity" (143). As before, my criticism here is not with Berry's thesis. I agree that we must be active and intentional concerning our relationship with transhuman nature in order to ensure the health and well-being of the world beyond our control, both for its own sake and for its ability to instruct us concerning our limits. However, by relying on this oppositional terminology, Berry once again reinscribes the old dualism by implying that nature and culture, wildness and domesticity, are separate and distinguishable.

He also creates problems in this essay by equating wildness with nature and distinguishing both from humanity, all, ironically, in an attempt to assert human beings' naturalness. At one point he asserts that "to be divided against nature, against wildness, . . . is a human disaster because it is to be divided against ourselves" (141). Later he again argues that "we need wilderness also because wildness—nature—is one of our indispensable studies" (146). Again, Berry's terminology is not up to the task at hand. The point he evidently wants to make—that humans are natural beings who have elements of the wild within them—is undercut by a vocabulary that presupposes the unnaturalness and nonwildness of humanity. For our words *do* insinuate that humans are "divided against nature, against wildness," since "nature" and "wild" are used almost exclusively to refer to the nonhuman, noncivilized world. Granted, this is the very perception Berry is working against in sentences like these, but by equating wildness with nature, then discussing humans, "ourselves," as outsiders responding to this relationship, he divides the very worlds he is trying to unite.

Examining this aspect of Berry's work in light of the place-space framework, it becomes clear that in spite of the poet's desire to overcome the modern human/nonhuman split, he at times relies on a vocabulary that for centuries has been implicated in creating and sustaining that very rift. Put simply, while Berry's writings consistently portray an attitude that prizes both place and space and recognizes the importance of their interaction, he at times slips into a language that intensifies the division between human and nonhuman worlds.

I am certainly not arguing that by employing terms like "place-making" and "space-consciousness" we can somehow overcome the centuries-old confusion regarding humans and our place in the natural world. The framework does, however, offer alternatives that give us a more precise lexicon with which to describe our efforts at finding a home in nature while simultaneously respecting its ultimate unknowability. For instance, Berry's earlier argument would have been much more consistent and compelling had he argued for, instead of "sanctioning" and "allowing for" wilderness, the importance of maintaining areas that produce an appreciation of the spatial qualities of the natural world. Likewise, had he warned against separating ourselves from that part of nature that produces space-consciousness, instead of separating ourselves from nature itself, he could have avoided this criticism.

I am also not arguing that place and space are exact corollaries for culture and nature (or civilization and wilderness). Berry, like other contemporary environmental writers, has recognized the inherent fallacy in discussing civilization and wilderness as if they describe distinct, opposing concepts. Serving as something of a bridge between past and future ideology and terminology, Berry has been able largely to transcend the flawed vocabulary and overcome many of the limitations of the older words so that we can think beyond those words and concepts. Yet the shortcomings in the terminology underlying his philosophy highlight the problems in our current way of discussing human-nature relations. Consequently, it seems logical that a new relational and nonoppositional vocabulary to discuss these conceptions would be appropriate, even necessary, at this time. In our attempts to allow our worldview to evolve and adjust to changing situations and knowledge about the world, the place-space terminology offers a great deal more precision and consistency than the problematic vocabulary we have traditionally employed.

CHAPTER THREE

Finding the Way Back

Joy Harjo

in the albuquerque airport
trying to find a flight
to old oraibi, third mesa
TWA
    is the only desk open
bright lights outline new york, chicago
and the third attendant doesn't know
that third mesa
is a part of the center
of the world
and who are we
just two indians
at three in the morning
trying to find a way back

and then i remembered
that time simon
took a yellow cab
out to acoma from albuquerque
a twenty five dollar ride
to the center of himself

3 AM is not too late
to find the way back

—Joy Harjo, "3 AM"

IN "DEER DANCER," from her 1990 volume *In Mad Love and War*, Musco-gee-Creek poet Joy Harjo blasts her reader with a barrage of images depicting the pain and frustration of contemporary Native American life. Relating a memory from a "bar in the middle of winter," the poet describes herself and her companions as "Indian ruins" gathered at "the bar of broken survivors, the club of shotgun, knife wound, of poison by culture" (5). She says she wants to describe the pain in detail but knows that "in this language there are no words for how the real world collapses." So instead, responding to a standard pickup line she overhears—"*What's a girl like you doing in a place like this?*"—the poet asks a question of her own: "That's what I'd like to know, what are we all doing in a place like this?" (6). This question, with its larger implications concerning contemporary Western civilization, is central to Harjo's work. Since her earliest poems she has grappled with the dilemmas, alienation, anger, and (at times) hopelessness of living "in a place like this."

In response, Harjo attempts to "go back" to what she calls "the mythic world." This response accords with the work of Wendell Berry in that Harjo demonstrates a keen sense of place- and space-consciousness. Yet she differs from Berry in how she addresses the rift between self and nature, for she views modern alienation as largely a verbal, cultural construct that she attempts to bypass by *going back*, not in the sense of regressing, but of recovering a worldview that is mindful of both place and space.

IN ORDER TO comprehend Harjo's ideal of going back, we must examine what she finds so unsettling about the contemporary world. A good point to begin is a passage from Carol Lee Sanchez's "More Conversations from the Nightmare," where the poet calls herself one of the

Urban Indians
feasting out of context
multilayered collages
of who we used to be. (Hobson 249)

Harjo too situates her work amid the numerous problems contemporary American Indians face as they interact with modern technological civilization and its resultant violence, poverty, alcoholism, and brutality. We observe these afflictions throughout her verse, in which speakers again and again decry the horrors endemic to this "land of nightmares" (*WWF* xv) that divorces her and her people from the nonhuman world and all it offers.

Harjo repeatedly names and explores the numerous divisions, divorces, and inconsistencies that mar the effort to live meaningfully at "the ragged end of this century" (*WWF* 30). In "Anchorage," for example, she writes of walking through the city and coming upon a Native homeless woman, describing her as

> someone's Athabascan
> grandmother, folded up, smelling like 200 years
> of blood and piss, her eyes closed against some
> unimagined darkness, where she is buried in an ache
> in which nothing makes
> sense. (*SHSH* 14)

This scene, epitomizing the worst of a meaningless modern existence with its disintegrated relationships and families, points out that the oppression of American Indians did not end at the completion of the Trail of Tears. As Harjo puts it, "The landscape of the late twentieth century is littered with bodies of our relatives" (*WWF* 19).

This littered landscape is part of what Harjo calls "the psychic wound of the Americas" (139). The wound has two primary sources, the first being a loss of roots and connection: humans live alienated lives, isolated from each other and from the other occupants of the planet. Harjo figures a world where "casual murder[s]" of immigrant taxi drivers are ordinary, everyday events (*WWF* 36); where the Ku Klux Klan lynches African Americans, both young and old, both male and female, and not in 1926, but in 1986, and not in Mississippi, but in California (*IML* 11–12); where an Ojibwa veteran returns to his country after fighting in Vietnam, only to discover "the destruction of his people by laws" (*WWF* 22). This is a world, put simply, that seems anything but home. In Tuanian terminology, it is a "place-less" void, and Harjo's is "a voice looking for a home" (Wiget 186).

The symbol of this placelessness—or "displacement," as Harjo calls it, conjuring historical as well as sociogeographical associations—is the contemporary American city, which she repeatedly invokes as "a wilderness of concrete and steel, made within a labyrinth of mind" and devoid of nonhuman nature ("Circular" 71). Nancy Lang has discussed the city in Harjo's work:

> On the one hand, after a first reading, Harjo may seem to be writing out of the city-as-subject tradition of American poets like Walt Whitman, Carl Sandburg, Hart Crane, and William Carlos Williams. On the other hand, her city landscapes do not reflect promise and optimistic excitement, as do many urban settings of earlier white male American poets. Rather, Harjo's cities resonate with Native American memories of an endless and ongoing memory of Eurocentric and genocidal social and political policies: war, forced removal, imposed education, racism, and assimilation. ("Twin Gods" 41–42)

In poems like "Anchorage," the city serves as an emblematic representation of the modern world; the poet "creates a uniquely surreal, yet frighteningly accurate and familiar picture of modern American cities and their alienated citizenry" (Lang 41).

One of the most prevalent synecdochal images of the modern American city is the honky-tonk bar, a recurrent locus in Harjo's poems. "Night Out" gives shape to vague characters who embody isolation while simultaneously attempting to escape it. The poem begins with the poet addressing these figures directly, writing that as a result of alcohol, they "are powerful horses . . . / not the wrinkled sacks of thin, mewing / spirit, that lay about the bar early in the day / waiting for minds and bellies." Then, in characteristic Harjo style, she offers a litany of subtle and not-so-subtle examples of the shackling frustration the bar-dwellers feel, concluding the poem — after identifying with the characters ("I have heard you in my ownself") — with lines that evoke their desperate struggle to escape their addictive conditions:

> Your hearts float out in cigarette
> smoke, and your teeth are broken and scattered in my hands.
> It doesn't end
> For you are multiplied by drinkers, by tables, by jukeboxes
> by bars.

You fight to get out of the sharpest valleys cut down into
the history of living bone.
               And you fight to get in.
You are the circle of lost ones
                  our relatives.
You have paid the cover charge thousands of times over
with your lives
            and now you are afraid
                       you can never get out. (*SHSH* 21)

Resistance poems like this one appear throughout Harjo's work, the poet narrating her people's efforts to escape "the sharpest valleys cut down into / the history of living bone." As she tells us in the opening lines of "Autobiography," her tribe, the Creeks, "were a stolen people in a stolen land. Oklahoma meant defeat" (*IML* 14).

The speaker in another poem addresses a mother so disconnected from her family that her sons are living "in another language / in Los Angeles / with their wives." She tells this mother, "Maybe it was the Christians' language / that captured you, / or the bones that cracked in your heart each / time you missed the aboriginal music that you / were" (*SHSH* 16). Time and again Harjo's poems lament the fact that modern society exists within a place-less world that is utterly not-home. And as Andrew Wiget points out, even when modern technological advancements—the telephone, for instance—appear to offer the opportunity for meaningful relationship, their connective powers falter; the speaker's voice travels through the wires but never reaches its desired destination (187). The voice becomes, in Harjo's words, "caught / shredded on a barbed wire fence / and flutters soundless / in the wind" (*WM* 52). Her phrasing—"flutters soundless"—conveys a profound disconnection, a relationship "shredded" by modern civilization, represented here by a barbed-wire fence.

Besides this placelessness, the other principal source of Harjo's "psychic wound" and its consequent modern problems is an ignorance of nature's wildness and humans' relationship to that wildness. Like Berry, Harjo contends that this ignorance results from an underdeveloped appreciation of space and leads to an arrogance that makes us feel and act as if we can control forces that are obviously beyond our control. A prime example of this concept is Harjo's prose poem "Autobiography," part of which I quoted above, with its message that despite the appearance that the country has been stolen, the land will continue to insert itself into human consciousness, even when we attempt to forget it. This poem provides a glimpse of the anger the poet feels regarding the development and commercialization of her wild "homeland." Harjo writes, "Last week I saw the river where the hickory stood; this homeland doesn't predict a legacy of malls and hotels. Dreams aren't glass and steel but made from the hearts of deer, the blazing eye of a circling panther." The following lines relate the consequences of attempting to tame those dreams and ignore the wildness of the natural world: "Translating [the dreams] was to understand the death count from Alabama, the destruction of grandchildren, famine of stories. I didn't think I could stand it" (*IML* 14). Genocide, the destruction of languages and dialects, the loss of stories: these are the unimaginable repercussions of greedily attempting to tame that which should remain wild. Whether Harjo is pointing to the destruction of actual American Indians or to a more metaphorical spiritual and psychological domestication that takes place in all people as a result of modern civilization, the consequences are devastating.

Condemnation of this psychological domestication pervades Harjo's work. Her introduction to *She Had Some Horses*, for example, tells of her father's causing "a scene when he butchered deer from bowhunting after hanging them from the one tree in our yard." She explains that this spectacle proved too much for the neighbors, since in their world, "large animals were not present except as packaged meat in the grocery store" (6). In the same piece, Harjo points out how quickly technology has replaced the unbridled imaginative power horses formerly held within the human mind. Now, rather than roaming wide-open spaces as symbols of our own and all of nature's wildness, horsepower exists only in cars or in trucks like Harjo's father's, while real horses are "restricted by asphalt roads and highways." We can observe actual horses from the road, but they are fenced in, "lop[ing] across patches of prairie often next to pumping oil wells, daring humans to consider a different road" (6).

For Harjo, this different road is often a route that (at least partially) by-passes a Western rationality that separates and limits. We see this in her mythological and fablelike prose poem "The Flood," which portrays the effects of the eradication of undomesticated wildness. The poem begins with an allusion to "the watermonster, the snake who lived at the bottom of the lake. He had disappeared in the age of reason, as a mystery that never happened." Writing about this poem, Harjo explains that

> embedded in Muscogee tribal memory is the creature the tie snake, a huge snake of a monster who lives in waterways and will do what he can to take us with him. He represents the power of the underworld.

> He is still present today in the lakes and rivers of Oklahoma and Alabama, a force we reckon with despite the proliferation of inventions that keep us from ourselves. (*WWF* 17)

Ultimately, as "The Flood" tells us, "the watersnake was a story no one told anymore. They'd entered a drought that no one recognized as drought, the convenience store a signal of temporary amnesia" (*WWF* 16). In the age of reason, the wildness and mystery of the watersnake have been replaced by tame and drought-produced "inventions"—for instance, the all-night minimart—that "keep us from ourselves," especially the wild, "spatial" parts of ourselves.

HARJO THEREFORE falls in line with Berry (and other ecopoets) in asserting that modern alienation is a symptom of a lost sense of place and space. But whereas Berry asserts that that alienation results primarily from a loss of connection to transhuman nature, and therefore advocates a literal and physical return to the land, Harjo emphasizes that much of this alienation is a verbal, cultural construct resulting from Anglo society and language. This is not to say that she ignores the very real consequences of modern alienation and prejudice, but rather that she implicates the larger, systemic patterns of linguistic and cultural oppression as primary instigators of such consequences. Consistently, as in "What Music," Harjo names modern Western rationality as the culprit that has severed people from the rest of the natural world. In that poem it is "the Christians' language," an analogue for Western consciousness, that divorced the mother not only from her sons but also from her true self and "the aboriginal music" that she was.

Harjo has directly addressed this issue of language's disconnecting effects. She states:

> My frustration with the language, particularly the English language, stems from anger with the colonization process in which the English language was a vicious tool. The colonizers knew what they were doing when they tried to destroy tribal languages, and which, infuriatingly, they were successful at in many instances. Language is culture, a resonant life form itself that acts on the people and the people on it. The worldview, values, relationships of all kinds—everything, in fact—is addressed in and through a language. ("Spectrum" 100)

Thus when English killed the tribal languages, Native individuals were separated from significant portions of their cultures—their "worldview, values, relationships."

Written language offers a different, if related, type of problem:

> I believe that written language was, in many ways, a de-evolution of the communication process. You lose human contact, context of time and place, and a sense of relationship. With written communication, you gain the ability to lie more easily. There is separation between the speaker and the reader/listener. There is less accountability. ("Spectrum" 100–101)

These casualties of written language—"human contact, context of time and place, and a sense of relationship"—are also what is lost as a result of ignoring what I am calling place. Hence written language, implies Harjo, can easily divorce humans from place.[1]

Sometimes, however, language is not the explicit culprit in Harjo's poetry; it often metonymically represents the broader concept of Western, Cartesian rationality. In "Backwards," for example, Harjo tells of seeing a "fallen moon" rising into the sky, a vision that then leads her to the memory of a dream of a white moon "torn / at the edges"; in the dream, "a whiteman with a knife cut pieces / away / and threw the meat / to the dogs" (*SHSH* 20). Harjo has said in an interview that in her poems the moon represents, among other things, "the memory of Earth" ("Weaving" 135). Thus when the whiteman in her dream cuts away parts of the moon, he cuts away a portion of her (already somewhat fragile) connection to the natural world. Through this metaphorical excision, perpetrated by language and Western rationality, humans are increasingly separated from the rest of nature, and thus modern "people in the towns and in the cities" learn "not to hear the ground as it [spins] around / beneath them" (*SHSH* 18).

Harjo has stated more than once that this verbally induced separation is actually an illusion. In an exchange with Bill Moyers, she asserts that an artist must "work to find . . . connections" during "these difficult times when the illusion of separation among peoples has become so clear." Moyers follows the conversational thread:

You said "illusion."
Because I think it *is* an illusion. I think this is more the shadow world than it is the real world.
This world of alienation and of separation is the shadow world?
Yes, but this shadow world is also *very* real. There are many wars going on all over the world and each of them is very real, and the losses people suffer because of them are very real. I don't mean to deny that at all.
And yet there is something underneath that the artist sees?
Yes, but I think artists always have to include what's apparent and real in that vision, even while we're always searching for what makes sense *beyond* the world. ("Ancestral" 40)

Notice here that Harjo asserts (with emphasis) that separation "*is* an illusion" as she simultaneously acknowledges that separation actually exists. Her point, sustained throughout her poetry, is that on the one hand, we are not separated from anything else; on the contrary, everything is related to everything else, with nothing existing outside of nature and its processes. On the other hand, when humans behave as if we *are* isolated from each other and the rest of nature, "the losses people [and nonpeople] suffer because of it are very real."

So ultimately Harjo manages to have her ontological cake and eat it too. Even though humans are essentially in relationship with the rest of nature, they can, at least in terms of consequences, divorce themselves from it as well. Put differently, the *illusion* of alienation can create *actual* alienation. For when we view ourselves as separated from nature, we cannot view the world as home or place; instead, our surroundings will be simply an "environment" and natural nonhuman entities nothing more than natural "resources." Likewise, it is difficult to maintain an awareness of the world's wildness from such an isolated vantage point.

To summarize, Harjo envisions a contemporary world that is violent, oppressive, and dehumanizing. Two primary sources for our social and philosophical ills are a loss of a sense of place—in other words a loss of connection to the world around us—and a loss of space-consciousness—an ignorance of the wildness within the world and ourselves. And all of these theoretical predicaments, along with their resultant sociocultural problems, result largely from Western society and language, which arrived when "the first thief . . . cross[ed] over / into the nation of the heart" ("Forgetting" *MTNW* 40). Harjo's primary response to this difficult and sometimes overwhelming modern situation is to challenge her readers (and herself) to "go back" to what she calls "the mythic world."[2]

HARJO SAID IN A 1992 interview that "probably each poem or story I write" deals with the "disrupting and disorienting" effects of modern "urban society," "with resolution coming through reassertion of traditional tribal identity and values" ("Spectrum" 108). The implication that repeatedly appears in her work is that this modern rift can be reconciled through memory. Harjo therefore admonishes her readers, in the title poem to her 2000 collection *A Map to the Next World*, "Keep track of the errors of our forgetfulness; the fog steals our children while we sleep" (19). People need to recall the mythic world when self and nature were not distinct entities, but rather one interdependent and symbiotic organism. Thus the word "back" appears throughout Harjo's poetry, as when in "3 AM" she speaks of "trying to find a way back" to "the center of the world," which she equates with the center of her self. Songs, words, stories, memories: all become vehicles to transport poet and readers back to a place of nonduality, where people have not experienced what she calls "the shame of forgetfulness" (*WWF* 57).[3]

Harjo has commented on the significance of memory—"the other-sight"

—in shaping the present world. Introducing *She Had Some Horses* (1997), she writes, "I come from a people who are taught to forget nothing. I believe that every thought, every word, every song or horse that existed makes a mural of existence that gives form to this one we find ourselves in" (7–8). The "mural of existence" is memory itself, and it is what literally gives form to our present world. As Harjo put it in an interview, "Memory for me becomes a big word. It's like saying 'world.' Memory is the nucleus of every cell; it's what runs, it's the gravity, the gravity of the Earth. In a way, it's like the stories themselves, the origin of the stories, and the continuance of all the stories. It's this great pool of knowledge and history that we live inside" ("Laughter" 138). It also connects Harjo to the past world, the one Calvin Martin calls "the Indian thoughtworld" and Morris Berman calls "enchanted," the one Paula Gunn Allen points to when she writes of tribespeople who acknowledge "the essential harmony of all things and see all things as being of equal value in the scheme of things, denying the opposition, dualism, and isolation (separateness) that characterize non-Indian thought" (56).

Poem after poem works toward this same insight, with Harjo holding up memory as the means to reconnect with the past world wherein self is not isolated from nature. She encourages her audience to remember "the way the stars entered your blood / at birth" (*SHSH* 16). And to the mother whose sons are living in another language, she remarks that "the stars return every night to call you back" (*SHSH* 16). Likewise, Harjo's recurring character Noni Daylight encounters intense displacement around city intersections, described as "desolate oceans of concrete"; but within these oceans the heartbeat of Noni's mother "is a ghostly track that follows her," luring her "back" (*SHSH* 37).

We see this pattern from her earlier "horse poems" to the recent Hawaiian lyrics in her 2002 *How We Became Human: New and Selected Poems, 1975–2001*; Harjo repeatedly asserts that her true self exists in a biosocial relationship with the natural world, and that she must go back, she must return, to that world in order to find herself. In "Song for the Deer and Myself to Return On," the speaker tells of waking and singing a song to call deer while she is hunting "something as magic as deer / in this city far from the hammock of my mother's belly." While the poem never defines what this magic "something" is, we know that it is wild and mysterious and that it represents whatever has been lost as a result of being divorced from the maternal source that offers relationship with the rest of the world. The good news is that the song is effective:

> It works, of course, and deer came into this room
> and wondered at finding themselves
> in a house near downtown Denver.

The bad news, however, is that as a result of the song and the singing, it is now not only the singer but also the deer who are "far from the hammock of my mother's belly." So the poet is left, along with the deer, "trying to figure out a song / to get them back, to get all of us back, / because if it works I'm going with them" (*IML* 30). As Patrick Murphy explains, "To reclaim the deer requires reclaiming the heritage in which the deer and the people played out their lives together, *and* realizing that heritage as cultural practice in the present-day world" (*LNO* 85).

Possibly the best example of Harjo's message is her well-known poem "Remember," which concludes with these lines:

> Remember you are all people and all people
> are you.
> Remember you are this universe and this
> universe is you.
> Remember all is in motion, is growing, is you.
> Remember language comes from this.
> Remember the dance language is, that life is.
> Remember. (*SHSH* 40)

In its prayerful, chantlike rhythm and its cumulative parallel catalogue, this poem exemplifies the frequency and intensity with which Harjo expresses her desire to find a way back to a world where people understand the reciprocity between themselves and the rest of the universe.

Viewing lines like these last ones, we could easily mistake Harjo's vision for a naively nostalgic desire to return to a prelapsarian world she imagines as existing before the Europeans arrived on the continent. While this nostalgia certainly informs and influences her vision, it is balanced within a fairly complex cosmography that distinguishes between going "back" and "going backward." Going backward, Harjo acknowledges, is impossible; doing so would be akin to overcoming exile, which, as Edward Said writes, is "the unhealable rift forced between a human being and a native place, between the self and its true home: its essential sadness can never be surmounted" (101). Going back, in contrast, means recuperating and maintaining an awareness of the past while allowing it to translate itself into present and future wisdom and insight. Stephen Whithed offers a description of Berry's work that applies equally well to Harjo's, which "places value not on a literal or historical return, which is impossible, but on the restoration of a traditional understanding that measures value by a mutual interdependence" between self and world (10).

In "Heartshed," for instance, Harjo addresses "the one who knows / the sound they call / 'in the beginning'" (*IML* 62). In this case "they" refers presumably to Euro-Americans, and the "sound" represents an awareness of a long-gone, pre-Edenic wholeness that was soon transformed into a world where people "understood the talk of animals, and spring was lean and hungry with the hope of children and corn" (*IML* 1). The person Harjo addresses has retained this awareness, even into our own times, recognizing that there once existed "the not-yet abyss of past and future" (*IML* 47). But as Harjo makes clear, returning to what "they" call "in the beginning" is not the same as regressing: "It doesn't mean going backward. / Our bones are built of spirals" (*IML* 62–63).

The spirals mentioned here are a recurring symbol in Harjo's work. They serve as an alternative architecture for her mythic return, replacing the more linear pecking order of the traditional chain-of-being myth. Harjo has compared her vortex, which she declares "a pattern for survival" (*SCW* 16) to the hierarchical system more often presented in traditional Christianity:

> I think where theologians get into trouble is that they're working out of a hierarchical structure. There's God sitting at the top of the world, in the image of a man, no women around in that trilogy of God the Father, Son, and Holy Ghost. I propose a different structure; it's not original but what I've learned from being around tribal peoples, and in my own wanderings. The shape is a spiral in which all beings resonate. The bear is one

version of human and vice versa. The human is not above the bear, nor is Adam naming the bear. ("Weaving" 127)

The spiral, then, is an alternate model for going back, for returning to a time of nonduality, and in "Heartshed" it is set against "going backwards." Our very bones, "built of spirals," are aware of this interrelationship.

Notice the key distinction between Harjo and Berry here, and the surprising similarity of the implications arising from the two visions. While the authors differ in their choice of geometrical symbols, the resulting visions both aim at an awareness of relationship with and respect for the natural world. Viewing the two poets through the lens of the place-space framework highlights this correspondence, as we see that despite the points where they so obviously diverge, the poets ultimately propose comparable visions, both of which make place and appreciate space.

Harjo's spirals also call to mind another of Berry's themes, the fluid boundaries existing between past, present, and future. As Laura Coltelli points out, the vortex, Harjo's "most successful figurative description of the proceeding of memory," travels in both temporal directions. Coltelli explains that "the spinning movement of the vortex . . . spirals down the tip while simultaneously expanding toward the future" (9).[4] For Harjo, therefore, a movement "back" into the past is simultaneously and paradoxically a movement into the future. As she says in an interview with Joseph Bruchac, "The way I see remembering, just the nature of the word, has to do with going back. But I see it in another way, too. I see it as occurring, not just going back, but occurring right now, and also future occurrence so that you can remember things in a way that makes what occurs now beautiful" ("Story" 24). Thus the energy within Harjo's poetry "provides nourishment for memory, which strives to retrace the past not as an inducement to curl inwards on oneself, as if it were a point in time without escape route, but rather as a dynamic process to reaffirm ancient heritages and proceed forward on a path of constant renewal" (Coltelli 9). Andrew Wiget echoes this thought, explaining that "memory and imagination move [Harjo's] voice from pole to pole, from here to there, from past to future" (189).

Harjo contrasts her own vision with that of what she calls "a contemporary, industrial-age-Euro-American sense of space and time in which there's only the present." Harjo asserts that this is "a very adolescent sense of time. There is no future or past when it comes right down to what I need and want right now" ("Weaving" 128). Her poetry, on the other hand, blurs temporal boundaries, as when she prays for someone "who can help me walk this thin line between the breathing / and the dead" (*IML* 9), or when Noni Daylight is able to "remember" the future (*SHSH* 46). As Harjo told Moyers:

> I don't see time as linear. I don't see things as beginning or ending. A lot of people have a hard time understanding native people and native patience —they wonder why we aren't out marching to accomplish something. There is no question that we have an incredible history, but I think to understand Indian people and the native mind you have to understand that we experience the world very differently. For us, there is not just *this* world, there's also a layering of others. Time is not divided by minutes and hours, and everything has presence and meaning within this land-scape of timelessness. ("Ancestral" 38–39)

According to Harjo, the past constantly breaks through into the present while also driving us toward the future. So in "The Field of Miracles" she points to the Leaning Tower of Pisa where "the stunning marble beckons you toward history, the tower caught on the edge of some unseen boundary between then and now" (*WWF* 55).

An extended example of Harjo's "landscape of timelessness" can be seen in "Grace," the opening poem of *In Mad Love and War*. The poem begins by describing the invasion of "stubborn memory" into the present moment, as the speaker is engaged in "the epic search for grace." She explains that "the haunting voices of the starved and mutilated" entered the current world and "broke fences, crashed our thermostat dreams," so that "we couldn't stand it one more time" (*IML* 1). Then, in the middle of "a town that never wanted us,"

> one morning as the sun struggled to break ice, and our dreams had found us with coffee and pancakes in a truck stop along Highway 80, we found grace.

> I could say grace was a woman with time on her hands, or a white buffalo escaped from memory. But in that dingy light it was a promise of balance.

We once again understood the talk of animals, and spring was lean and hungry with the hope of children and corn.

Notice the temporal fusion here, that the speaker and her companions discover grace within an ordinary, present moment over coffee and pancakes, in response to past memories and with "a promise of balance" in the future. Yet Harjo does not conclude the poem in this state of grace: "I would like to say, with grace, we picked ourselves up and walked into the spring thaw. We didn't; the next season was worse. You went home to Leech Lake to work with the tribe and I went south." But the encounter with grace—Harjo's trip "back"—does not forsake her completely. The concluding lines of the meditation stress the power the experience still holds. She addresses her friend, Wind Welch, in the final sentences: "And, Wind, I am still crazy. I know there is something larger than the memory of a dispossessed people. We have seen it." Hence, while "back" may not be a permanent destination, Harjo's *journey* back collapses temporal boundaries and leaves her with a vision of a time when people could still talk with animals, "the ancestors who never left" (*IML* 6).[5]

So, ultimately, Harjo seeks to diminish barriers—mental, physical, temporal—that separate humans from each other and from the natural world, thereby to return "back" to a non- or less-dualistic world. As Kathleen McNerney Donovan puts it, Harjo's poetry "seeks a unity of thought with form. It is about breaking down boundaries between people, between the divided self, between genres, between text and life" (61). In this unifying process of going back—in remembering, in telling the old stories—people become more capable of learning once again how to connect with place and appreciate space.

THE QUESTION thus becomes how, in going back, Harjo is able to create place- and space-consciousness in her poetry. Whereas Berry becomes a place-maker by returning to the actual land and connecting with it, Harjo's return is (primarily) an imaginative one that allows her to reclaim what language and Western culture have threatened to take from her. She has stated, almost explicitly, that what I am calling place-making is the purpose of her poetry: "I've been especially involved in the struggles of Indian peoples to maintain a place and culture in this precarious age. My poetry has everything to do with this" (Smith and Allen 24). My argument here is that Harjo's place-making creates a poetry of what she calls a "land-based language" that contains a certain "knowing of that landscape, as something alive with personality, breathing. Alive with names, alive with events" ("Circular" 70–71).

The goal, says Harjo, is to write a poem that becomes "a home, sometimes with a glimpse, an eye toward the story of origin, or a place for the human understanding of a hummingbird" ("Landscape" 76). Therefore, the processes of going back and place-making are intertwined; in order to recover a sense of place we must remember and return to what we have known in the past. She writes, in "Skeleton of Winter," that even at times that are "almost too dark for vision," "there is still memory, / the other-sight / and still I see." She articulates the bodily essence of memory, equating memory with her very self:

A tooth-hard rocking
in my belly comes back,
something echoes
all forgotten dreams,
          in winter.
I am memory alive
          not just a name
but an intricate part
of this web of motion,
meaning: earth, sky, stars circling
my heart. . . . (*SHSH* 30–31)

It is memory, for Harjo, that connects her to everything else; memory makes place, keeping her aware of her relationship to all things. In the words of Coltelli, Harjo's poems "have come to form an integral part of the heritage through which the wisdom and experience of a people are handed down from one generation to another; they embody the sense of belonging to a community, to a land, to a past that flows without discontinuity into the present" (8).

As emblems of memory and storytelling, horses serve in Harjo's poetry as symbols of the power of tribal myths and heritage. She writes that horses were present in images and paintings in her childhood home, and "in the myths and history of the tribe and the state of Oklahoma. They also ran through my dreams as if to thread my life together when it appeared broken, unthreadable" (*SHSH* 6). An unthreadable world is a placeless one. Thus to go back is to thread life together, to make place. For here, at the end of the twentieth century, we're "naked but for the stories we have of each other" ("Reconciliation" *WWF*).

In her preface to *Secrets from the Center of the World*, a book of prose poems coauthored with the photographer Stephen Strom, Harjo emphasizes the significance of recognizing a relationship to place:

> All landscapes have a history, much the same as people exist within cultures, even tribes. There are distinct voices, languages that belong to particular areas. There are voices inside rocks, shallow washes, shifting skies; they are not silent. And there is movement, not always the violent motion of earthquakes associated with the earth's motion or the steady unseen swirl through the heavens, but other motion, subtle, unseen, like breathing. A motion, a sound, that if you allow your own inner workings to stop long enough, moves into the place inside you that mirrors a similar landscape; you too can see it, feel it, hear it, know it. (1)

Harjo asserts that Strom's photographs "lead you to that place"; she says that the pictures "emphasize the 'not-separate' that is within and that moves harmoniously upon the landscape." Like Harjo's poems, Strom's photographs make place by helping us recognize the "not-separate" that exists between ourselves and our world.

Strom and Harjo's place-making is balanced by a space-consciousness, also achieved through a movement back. In a Tuanian sense, Harjo almost never speaks of making place without offering the other, spatial side of the coin. She recognizes that whatever we do to make place, we must acknowledge that our supposed control over the world is illusory. Therefore, after speaking of Strom's ability to make place in his photography, Harjo explains that the photographs are not separate from the land, or larger than it. Rather they gracefully and respectfully exist inside it. Breathe with it. The world is not static but inside a field that vibrates. The whole earth vibrates. Stephen Strom knows this, sees this, and successfully helps us to remember. (1)

When we remember, we go back, and just as doing so helps create place, it also serves to confirm the importance of "gracefully and respectfully" heeding the spatial quality, the vibrating relatedness, of the world around us.

This recognition that we are not separate from the land also offers balance to a society that has become too "civilized," consequently losing any connection with the wilder, less domesticated parts of nature and ourselves. (As a result of our ignorance of space, writes Harjo, "even the chickens . . . [have] become too civilized"; now they must dream of "the one place they remembered how to fly over the walls of chicken wire" [*WWF* 58].)

"Deer Dancer" communicates the relationship between going back and appreciating space. Harjo's speaker tells her listener of her kinship to the natural world, explaining it as a product of the connective ability of memories, songs, and stories. Then, after setting up the relationship between the people, the speaker's self, her memory, the gods, and the deer, the poem closes with an adamant declaration concerning our ability to understand the world around us:

> I don't care what you say. The deer is no imaginary tale
> I have created to fill this house because you left me.
> There is more to this world than I have ever let on
> to you, or anyone. (*IML* 29)

Harjo's speaker acknowledges and respects the vastness of "this world." For whatever reason — either because what she knows is unutterable or because she chooses not to verbalize her knowledge — the speaker embraces the unnameable and respects its unutterable, spatial quality.

One character who embodies Harjo's appreciation of space is Noni Daylight, the young Native woman who lives recklessly and loves passionately, who "longs for the totality of loving, the ecstasy of union" (Wiget 187). Noni "tracks the / heart sound on the streets of Albuquerque" (*SHSH* 37), experimenting with LSD and considering suicide because she "needs the feel of danger, / for life" (*SHSH* 46). She is related to Harjo's horses "who laughed too much," "who threw rocks at glass houses," "who licked razor blades" (*SHSH* 63). Lang and Wiget both provide useful readings of the Noni Daylight poems, arguing that Noni is in fact Harjo's "other-self" with whom she negotiates, and ultimately accepts, in a paradoxical, contradictory, yet healing dialogue. In "She Remembers the Future," Noni speaks with her "other-self," the more cautious, poetic persona, who "whispers to herself" warnings and admonitions. Noni responds, and in her question ridicules this other-self for her preoccupation with "safety": "Should I dream you afraid / so that you are forced to save yourself? // Or should you ride colored horses / into the cutting edge of the sky / to know // that we're alive / we are alive" (*SHSH* 46). In all her recklessness and destructiveness, therefore, Noni represents the space side of Harjo's Tuanian binary, the yin to the poet's yang, the Dionysian to her Apollonian.

Another space-conscious character frequently appearing in Harjo's work is the trickster, often in the form of Crow or Rabbit in Muscogee mythology.[6] Harjo has said that in her work "Crow represents a kind of renegade, sort of a free spirit, independent, a wise trickster—a speaker of asides in this tricky unraveling, punctuating the drama, keeping track" ("Landscape" 78). Crow offers what Harjo calls the "laughter of absolute sanity that might sound like someone insane" but that "in the middle of all the tension and destruction" is actually "the voice of sense" ("Laughter" 142). Rabbit often plays a similar role, as we see in "The Book of Myths," where the poet sees "Rabbit sobbing and laughing / as he shook his dangerous bag of tricks / into the mutiny world on that street outside Hunter [College]" (*IML* 55). So when Harjo faces the horror of the modern world, she often looks to the trickster for a model of how to respond: "Like Coyote, like Rabbit, we could not contain our terror and clowned our way through a season of false midnights. We had to swallow the town with laughter, so it would go down easy as honey" (*IML* 1). Consequently, Harjo herself often plays the trickster role, challenging and disrupting traditional Western ways of thinking and knowing by questioning reality and the way we ordinarily perceive time and space. As she says, "Europe has gifted us with inventions, books and the intricate mechanics of imposing structures on the earth, but there are other means to knowledge and the structuring of knowledge that have no context in the European mind" (*SHSH* 7).

Emblematic of these "other means" is what we might call the postgeneric quality of Harjo's verse, which we witness in her refusal to limit herself to a certain type of poetic expression. In fact, rather than postgeneric, we might better use "pregeneric," for, as Arnold Krupat explains, "Traditional Native American literary forms were not—and, in their contemporary manifestations usually are not—as concerned about keeping fiction and fact or poetry and prose distinct from one another. It is the distinction between truth and error rather than that between fact and fiction that seems more interesting to native expression" (59). Indeed, viewing only Harjo's collections of poetry—in other words, excluding the more conventional prose writings and interviews she has published—we find a remarkably wide array of genres and modes, including traditional lyrics, prose poems, myths, ceremonies, and even analytical discussions of other poems. Clearly, generic limitations matter little, if at all, to Harjo. Like Leslie Marmon Silko's *Storyteller*, with its mixture of short stories, poems, photographs, and legends, and like N. Scott Momaday's *The Way to Rainy Mountain*, with its powerful combination of poetic, historical, and mythic voices, Harjo's work displays a freedom that often defies, or better yet ignores, generic and formalistic convention.

Accordingly, instead of an emphasis on individual subjectivity, Harjo's work emphasizes a radical *intersubjectivity*, with human and nonhuman figures repeatedly fusing into other bodies and psyches. As we have already seen, an element of the uncanny is woven throughout Harjo's work: a deer may turn into a woman, a person into the wind, a bird into the sun. Jenny Goodman explores Harjo's surrealism in reference to "Crossing Water," a poem that "is at once poetic and political" and offers "the validation of ways of knowing that are simply denied in mainstream American culture" (Goodman 44). "Crossing Water" opens with the lines

I return like a detective to the dance floor in New York, or was it
    someplace

else invented to look like October? I turn back to a music the d.j. never
played because the room was too blue for falling angels. Nothing by
   Aretha,
nothing by chance. A woman chased by spirits kept asking you to dance,
made a gift of her hands. I add her to the evidence: we were there. She
   was
a witness but I don't have her name. Or yours or mine, or was the shift in
axis an event in the imagination? (*IML* 46)

In her discussion of this poem, Goodman writes:

> Clearly, we cannot read within the conventions of the personal lyric,
> which claims to tell us a story that "really happened." And yet the poem
> presents "evidence" that the event is in fact real for the poet-speaker, ac-
> cording to rules of evidence that do not match those of the personal lyric
> or of our dominant culture, the latter still giving authority to the positiv-
> ist language of science and technology and the "expert" language of the
> think-tank professional and network newscaster. This poem's evidence
> and witnesses are of a different order than those the culture recognizes
> as "real" in its courtrooms, for instance. . . . This poem insists that *poetic*
> evidence, *spiritual* evidence, is valid. (45)

Within this insistence lies a direct challenge, no less seditious than those
posed by Crow or Rabbit, to traditional Western thinking and its reliance
on the five senses and stable subjectivities.[7]

The most recent manifestation of Harjo's space-consciousness in her po-
etry and her life is her fascination with music, particularly jazz. Over the last
several years Harjo and her bands Poetic Justice and The Real Revolution
have traveled the country performing her poems set to instrumental music.
Within her written work, this enchantment with music began to appear
most prominently in her 1990 volume *In Mad Love and War*, which is full
of references to jazz legends like John Coltrane, Charlie Parker, and Billie
Holiday. Most of these references suggest music's ability to remind us of a
world that resists control or containment. In "Original Memory," for ex-
ample, Harjo writes of "flying on a saxophone," "trying to leap past 4/4 time

to understand it." She ends the poem with the question "And who are we to make sense of this slit of impossible time?" (*IML* 48).

Music offers the means to bypass certain rational and logical tendencies that usually hinder us from recognizing what she calls "the more spiritual sense of the world." Harjo has implied in an interview that her music, which she describes as a "soulmate" to her poetry (*MTNW*), offers counterforce against the pull into hyperrationality. When asked about the influence of jazz on her forms, she responded:

> Well, that wasn't conscious. I think it's coming out of playing the saxophone. I realized recently that I took it up exactly when I entered academe. I don't feel like I've become an academic but if you're going to be in that place, certainly it's going to rub off on you. [laughter] ("In Love" 118)

The same goes for Harjo's poetry. She says that when she first began writing, she "started out knowing definitely what I wanted to begin and end with, or one particular image that I wanted to stay with." But speaking as a more mature and (I would add) space-conscious poet, she says, "Now I feel that my poems have become travels *into* that other space" (Moyers 38). As she puts it elsewhere, "Each time I write I am in a different and wild place, and travel toward something I do not know the name of. Each poem is a jumping-off edge and I am not safe" ("Ordinary Spirit" 268). By embracing this "wild place" and its inherent danger, Harjo suggests, she can more healthfully deal with the unknown, in effect by acknowledging her basic inability to control the world around her.

The concepts surrounding Harjo's space-consciousness as I am describing it here are largely summed up and exemplified in her poem "Bird," an homage to Charlie Parker that contains these lines:

> All poets
> understand the final uselessness of words. We are chords to
>
> other chords to other chords, if we're lucky, to melody. The moon
> is brighter than anything I can see when I come out of the theater,
>
> than music, than memory of music, or any mere poem. (*IML* 21)

Harjo makes clear here that language, even when used to create poems, is ultimately futile. For even the poets themselves represent only segments of life, which they hope add up to some sort of music—"chords to other chords to other chords." And the natural world, symbolized here by the moon, transcends the poet's attempts to capture it in song, music, poetry, and even memory, all of which represent what Harjo elsewhere calls "constructs." Thus, as she tells us later in this same poem, "to survive is sometimes a leap into madness," for madness is wild and uncontrollable, and when we recognize the limits to our ability to gain any sort of mastery over the world, then we appreciate this madness, this wildness, this space.

ULTIMATELY, THEN, Harjo's vision recognizes both place and space and achieves their interplay on two distinct but related levels. The first, more conspicuous level has to do with a simple coexistence and interaction between place and space. Harjo and Strom have offered a good example of this process in *Secrets from the Center of the World*, where poems and photographs come together both to make place—by helping us view the natural world (in this case the Navajo desert) almost as a personality with whom we can interact—and to appreciate space—by pointing out the immensity within the world's beauty, a magnitude we cannot fully fathom. Coltelli discusses this concept, without using the terms place and space, contending that in *Secrets*,

> Harjo weaves the web of a passionate dialogue with Stephen Strom's outstanding photographs. The essence of Strom's shots lies in eschewing any facile reliance on the spectacular depth of perspective of the wide open spaces characteristic of the American landscape, impressive though such a setting may be. Refraining from the sometimes hackneyed scenic depth shots, the vast expanse is instead condensed into a miniature dimension, so that our eye, instead of losing itself in a cliché of immensity, is obliged to look at it with focus on the particular. And it is on these particulars that Harjo's poetry centers, intensely seeking to affirm that the knowledge of physical roots is the knowledge of spiritual belonging. (3)

Just as Strom's photographs are able to communicate both the space-conscious "vast expanse" and the place-centered "focus on the particular," so Harjo's work recognizes the threads linking physicality and spirituality, as well as place and space. As Coltelli puts it at another point, Harjo's poems are "projections of different worlds that absorb into their being the experience of mystery yet can be controlled by a culture because they have been blended into the ancient stories" (8). The "mystery" and "culture" that join forces in the poems and the photographs are analogues for space and place, and both challenge us to learn to interpret what Harjo elsewhere calls "the language of the land" (*MTNW* 19).

On another, less explicit level, a more mystical interaction occurs between place and space in Harjo's work. Reading Harjo, one senses that other worlds do indeed exist, worlds beyond our ability to understand them. These mythical, mysterious worlds are the domain of space. Yet at the same time, Harjo's poems naturalize these spatial worlds, presenting them as if they were our ordinary, everyday environments, as if they were nothing that should surprise us. In doing so, she creates a strange synergism that actually presents space as *a type of place*, one that a person might inhabit as home.

We observe this process in "Deer Ghost," as Harjo's speaker manages to create place within a story by rendering a tale in which magic and mystery seem as ordinary and believable as a jukebox or a pool table. Experiencing the poem's narrative, we are able to imagine the magical deer dancer and her red dress as she appears:

> Of course we noticed when she came in. We were Indian ruins. She was the end of beauty. No one knew her, the stranger whose tribe we recognized, her family related to deer, if that's who she was, a people accustomed to hearing songs in pine trees, and making them hearts. (*IML* 29)

Even coming from a Western, logocentric perspective, most readers have no trouble entering this world and accepting that the beautiful woman is actually kin to deer, or that her human relatives can communicate in some way with pines. We have read our Coleridge. Yet Harjo's request is more than that we willingly suspend disbelief; she asks us to view her alternate world as real, just as real as the world we perceive through our five senses. Then she goes a step further. She asks us not only to *acknowledge* worlds beyond our rational knowledge but to view them as attractive places, as places with much to offer our logical, safe, understood, and understandable existence. Drawing on Kristeva's "semiology of the uncanny," Elaine A. Jahner explains that Deer Woman challenges all that we know, "destructuring and restructuring all of our libidinal energies and . . . unleashing the creativity" of those she calls, including the audience of the poem (169). Harjo asks that we understand, along with the bar denizens, that as Deer Woman danced, "she was the myth slipped down through dreamtime. The promise of feast we all knew was coming. The deer crossed through knots of a curse to find us." Such is the experience of space.

In the poem's conclusion, then, Harjo makes a move that transforms the entire process:

> The music ended. And so does the story. I wasn't there. But I imagined her like this, not a stained red dress with tape on her heels but the deer who entered our dream in white dawn, breathed mist into pine trees, her fawn a blessing of meat, the ancestors who never left. (*IML* 29)

In acknowledging that she "wasn't there," Harjo places herself back in our world, the "real" world, as if to concede that the tale is simply a make-believe fantasy, a fable with a moral at the end. However, with the word "but" Harjo again reverses direction, elevating the level and force of her tone to a proclamation. In her statement "I imagined her like this," Harjo in effect says, "This *is* the way it happened, because my imagination, deeply rooted in my memory, sees it this way; and what I remember is real." With such conviction Harjo displays her vision, offering it as an engaging invitation to join her in her spatial world. The poem therefore makes place even within the space, for Deer Woman "frames the experience of the uncanny," molding it into a "cultural expression by giving it a narrative frame and a legendary path to pursue through history" (Jahner 169). Within space Harjo has made place.

DESPITE THEIR numerous and obvious differences, Harjo and Berry are strikingly similar in terms of both their presentation of the problems associated with modernity and their response to it. Both lament our modern alienation, and name, as the leading contributor to it, Western civilization's historic decision to sever itself from the natural world. Both point to our loss of place and space (although neither uses this precise terminology) as symptomatic and causative of these problems, and both strive to restore connection to place and appreciation for space through their writings. And both do so by looking to past wisdom and insight, while stressing that past, present, and future are always and intensely related, as are place and space.

However, as I have noted, Harjo's specific response differs from Berry's, which centers (in Lionel Basney's words) on "turn[ing] away from mere vision, or theory, to the application of theory as the actual means of his existence in the world" (140). Thus Berry writes, "I am endlessly in need of the work of poets who have been concerned with living in place, the life of a place, long-term attention and devotion to a settled home and its natural household, and hence to the relation between imagination and language and a place" (*SBW* 88). As Andrew Angyal puts it, for Berry, poetry, "by its very nature, . . . is local and regional, inhabiting a particular physical landscape rather than a universal landscape of the mind" (117). Harjo, on the other hand, focuses less on actually walking the rows of the field than on knowing the myths and history of her past, thereby recovering the wisdom that views the landscape "as something alive with personality, breathing. Alive with names, alive with events" ("Circular" 70–71). And as for space-consciousness, Harjo's poetry, instead of pointing to the forested wilderness beyond the farm as Berry's does, at times aims at a transrationality, and at other times links itself with such nonverbal expressions as photography and music, highlighting poetry's inability to grasp the ineffable. Instead of advocating a *physical* return to an agrarian relationship with the land, Harjo advocates a spiritual and *metaphysical* return that will alter our thinking about that relationship.

These themes are encapsulated in "Wolf Warrior," a poem that offers a challenge that recurs throughout Harjo's work as well as throughout ecopoetry. In this poem the speaker, walking through Washington, D.C., offers a story to a friend who is on her way to "argue a tribe's right to water" at "what used to be the Department of War." She begins her narrative and we quickly perceive it to be a frame around another tale, for she explains that "an old Cherokee who prizes wisdom above the decisions rendered by departments of justice told me this story." The old Cherokee's story, "which isn't Cherokee but a gift given to him from the people in the north," tells of a young hunter who is visited by "a wolf walking toward camp on her hind legs." As she is welcomed by the young hunter and his dogs (who "were awed to see their ancient relatives and moved over to make room for them at the fire"), the wolf motions for her companions to join her. At this point another story is told, as the hunter and the wolf converse:

> He knew this meeting was unusual and she concurred, then told the story of how the world as they knew it had changed and could no longer support the sacred purpose of life. Food was scarce, pups were being born deformed and their migrations which were in essence a ceremony for renewal were restricted by fences. The world as all life on earth knew it would end and there was still time in the circle of hope to turn back the destruction. (*WWF* 46)

The wolf explains: "That's why they had waited for him, called him here from the town a day over the rolling hills, from his job constructing offices for the immigrants." Then she and her companions depart, saying, "We have others with whom to speak and we haven't much time." The poem closes with the following paragraphs:

> The story burned in the heart of this human from the north and he told it to everyone who would listen, including my elder friend who told it to me one day over biscuits and eggs.

> The story now belongs to you too, and much as pollen on the legs of a butterfly is nourishment carried by the butterfly from one flowering to another, this is an ongoing prayer for strength for us all. (*WWF* 44–47)

This "ongoing prayer" is something of a synopsis of the converging elements of Harjo's poetry. It honestly and unflinchingly presents the perilous circumstances that she views as the culminating consequences of centuries of Western "civilization." Then it calls on its audience to respond to these circumstances and to change them, offering a series of place- and space-conscious challenges: to make our environment a home people care for and to which they feel they belong; to expand our present ways of perceiving the world and remove restricting fences that prevent us from imagining different possibilities; and to pass along the story of destruction as well as the healing truth.

The strategy Harjo employs to accomplish all of this is to go back, using memory and multiple narratives. Notice that the poem begins as *a story* and quickly becomes *stories*, moving sequentially through several layers as the multivoiced narratives lead from one to the next. Originating from the reader's perspective on the outer surface of the text, the poem spirals inward to the activist addressed by the poet, then to the poet herself, and on to the old Cherokee, to the young hunter, and finally to the wolf, whose tale forms the kernel of the poem. In effect, the poem, with its series of storytelling events, develops into a model for going back, as one individual's vision is shared with another and another and ultimately becomes communal, tribal, with the potential to effect changes in the perspectives and practices of those who hear it and accept the responsibility of passing it along.

CHAPTER FOUR

Both Sides of the Beautiful Water | Mary Oliver

To live in this world

you must be able
to do three things:
to love what is mortal;
to hold it

against your bones knowing
your own life depends on it;
and, when the time comes to let it go,
to let it go.

—Mary Oliver, "In Blackwater Woods"

THERE IS NO QUESTION that Mary Oliver is the least overtly political of the writers I examine in this book. Her poetry rarely turns polemical, and on an initial read one might assume her to be simply one of the latest traditional nature poets, gifted poetically, but not apparently energized by any overt environmental or political fervor. However, as much as anyone writing today, Oliver demonstrates in her work a deep awareness of the principal characteristics and themes that dominate contemporary ecopoetry. Describing what he calls Oliver's "ecological" imagination, John Elder writes that she "understands the recycling of life through an ecosystem and also registers this reality as a psychological and emotional fact" (221). And as Oliver herself explained in a 1991 article for the magazine *Sierra*, her poetry proceeds from a conscious and purposeful environmental awareness:

> To me it is madness to set art apart from other social and spiritual endeavors. Writing that does not influence the reader is art that sleeps, and misses the point. Not infused with conscious intention, nor built upon polemic, a poem will inevitably reflect the knowledge and the outlook of the writer. Before we move from recklessness into responsibility, from selfishness to a decent happiness, we must want to save our world. And in order to want to save the world we must learn to love it—and in order to love it we must become familiar with it again. That is where my work begins, and why I keep walking, and looking. ("Among Wind and Time" 34)

What Oliver presents in her deceptively simple poems, resulting from her walking and looking, is a complex perspective on the relationship between the environmentally aware artist and her nonhuman subjects.

When asked if he at times felt his voice "coming not from the human culture but instead from the silent herds being destroyed by that human culture," W. S. Merwin replied by warning against presumption but allowing that "it's very important to remain open to that possibility, to welcome it, and to evoke it if possible." He went on to discuss how a poet can indeed speak for the nonhuman other:

> The nearest thing I can imagine to what I would think of as a sound or even healthy approach and attitude toward existence as a whole (as distinct from the endless separation of the human species from the rest of exis-

tence that leads to evaluating the one at the expense of the other) — would be Blake's "How do you know but ev'ry Bird that cuts the airy way, / Is an immense world of delight, clos'd to your senses five?" It works both ways, one both can be and can never be the bird. ("Fact Has Two Faces" 329–330)

With that sentiment in mind, and to set up my analysis of Oliver's ecopoetry, I begin with a reading of one of her most representative poems, "The Osprey," from her 1997 *West Wind*.

The speaker of the poem closely describes an osprey's retrieval of a fish from a body of water, then stands looking at the spot of the action. The speaker says, "Then I walked away. / Beauty is my work, / but not my only work." She later returns to the water and, in the close of the poem, becomes the protagonist of the drama she has just depicted:

I mean, I was swimming for my life —
and I was thundering this way and that way
in my shirt of feathers —
and I could not resolve anything long enough

to become one thing
except this: the imaginer.
It was inescapable
as over and over it flung me,

without pause or mercy it flung me
to both sides of the beautiful water —
to both sides of the knife. (21)

In this poem we get the quintessential Oliver: the intense observer who identifies with her nonhuman subjects to such an extent that she somehow enters their world, becoming for a moment those subjects. As she explains, beauty — the strict observation of the world's beauty — is her work, but not exclusively. Oliver's poetry also reveals her passionate identification with those she describes, as she, the imaginer, manages to insert herself into another's world, even its consciousness. Yet in Oliver's work the imaginer never ceases to be — or to know that she is — *only* the imaginer, and not the actual osprey or the silver fish. In Merwin's words, she both can be and can never be the bird.

In her latest poetry, especially that of the last decade or so, Oliver consistently shifts from one side "of the beautiful water," in her role as strict observer of beauty, to the other side, in her role as imaginer of an alternate consciousness. Here I want to explore Oliver's shifting between the two sides of the water. Like Berry and Harjo, she laments the modern divorce between humans and the rest of nature, and this shifting is her principal response to it. Oliver's poetry proceeds out of a phenomenological worldview centered in the body's fundamental relatedness to the rest of nature. As such, it rests on a place-centered poetics that allows her momentarily to enter the consciousness of her natural subjects. As a result of her awareness of this bodily connection, Oliver frequently and intentionally employs the pathetic fallacy. But she does so in a highly self-conscious manner that signifies her awareness of her inability actually to speak for nature, since she is merely "the imaginer." Thus her poetics are space-centered as well. In other words, Oliver's response to the dualistic crisis proceeds out of a deep desire to play the role of related participant in the world she observes; she tempers her excitement over a perceived biological relationship, however, with this ever-present awareness that real connection between herself and the rest of the natural world most often takes place only as an act of imagination. Thus, like Berry and Harjo, Oliver makes place (in her desire for relationship) while maintaining (in her self-consciousness) an intense appreciation for space. This place- and space-conscious response highlights many similarities between Oliver and the other ecopoets as well as a significant difference: she displays a more self-reflexive awareness concerning the difficulties involved in overcoming modern alienation.

LIKE THE THEORISTS and ecopoets I have discussed thus far, Oliver has throughout her career called attention to the split between humanity and nonhuman nature. Like Harjo, Oliver foregrounds the fact that people have allowed language and rationality to separate them from the rest of the natural world. As she puts it in "The Shark," "The connections have broken" (*DW* 72). Thus in "Spring Azures," for example, she jealously describes the blue butterflies as they "rise and float away into the fields," then thinks of "the great bones of my life [that] feel so heavy," and of all the separating and differentiating elements of her human self, "the opposable thumbs, the kneecaps, / the mind clicking and clicking" (*NS* 8). This "clicking and clicking" mind, emblematic of humans' overreliance on rationality, repeatedly shows up in Oliver's work, as she laments that people are estranged from the rest of nature and require that "the gods" use nature to "shake us from our sleep" (*WDWK* 40).

In "One or Two Things," for instance, Oliver writes of her own preoccupation with the future, a (harmful) central characteristic of modern human consciousness, clearly not shared by our nonhuman counterparts. In the poem the dirt, the dog, the crow, and the frog all have only one simple message: "*now.*" The poet, on the other hand, obsesses about the future, the concept of *forever* lodged in her mind "like a sharp iron hoof." Throughout her poetry, Oliver asserts that her own preoccupation with the future, and with philosophical questions concerning meaning and purpose, prevent her from fully experiencing the world around her, unlike other natural beings.

Consequently, Oliver again and again expresses her envy of her nonhuman counterparts' ability to be what she calls "perfect," that is, being able to live contentedly, in the present, without the constraints of human civilization and consciousness. We see this perfection repeatedly: woodland animals live "where life has no purpose / and is neither civil nor intelligent" (*NS* 7); "wild, amoral, reckless, peaceful flowers" fill the hillsides (*NS* 43); blossoms are eager "to be wild and perfect for a moment, before they are / nothing, forever" (*NS* 21); and a gull's life represents "the white and silky trumpet of nothing. / Here is the beautiful Nothing, body of happy, / meaningless fire, wildfire, shaking the heart" (*WW* 40). "Amoral," "reckless," "neither civil nor intelligent," "the beautiful Nothing," "meaningless fire": these phrases declare Oliver's admiration for the "perfection" she observes in the natural world. And more often than not, at least a tinge of jealousy appears in the midst of the poet's admiration, as we clearly hear in Oliver's description of three egrets that are "unruffled . . . by the laws of their faith not logic" to the extent that they open their wings "softly" and step over "every dark thing" (*AP* 19 – 20). In what she calls the birds' "faith in the world," Oliver points to a feature she admires but cannot attain. This "faith" serves not as a future-oriented belief system, but instead as an acceptance of and fidelity to the moment-by-moment processes of life.

The title character from "The Turtle" further exemplifies this being-in-nature concept of "faith not logic." The speaker in this poem praises the nest-building turtle for "her patience, her fortitude, / her determination to complete / what she was born to do." The poet then checks herself, realizing that the turtle "doesn't consider / what she was born to do. / She's only filled / with an old blind wish." The speaker explains that this preconscious, instinctual "old blind wish" is actually what connects the turtle to her world and her home, and that "she can't see / herself apart from the rest of the world / or the world from what she must do / every spring." The poet speculates that the turtle doesn't merely dream, but actually "knows" that "she is a part of the pond she lives in, / the tall trees are her children, / the birds that swim above her / are tied to her by an unbreakable string" (*DW* 57–58). This is the natural "perfection" to which Oliver repeatedly points: the turtle's unconsidered, blind awareness that she is "part of the pond she lives in." Whereas in the human world "the connections have broken," the turtle is tied to her world "by an unbreakable string."

As another example of this contrast, consider the opening lines of "Landscape," a rhetorical question concerning the lack of ambition exhibited by nonhuman natural entities: "Isn't it plain the sheets of moss, except that / they have no tongues, could lecture / all day if they wanted about // spiritual patience?" Having no desire to change their situation, the sheets of moss represent perfection for Oliver. She reinforces this theme throughout the poem, concluding by describing crows that "burst up into the sky—as though / all night they had thought of what they would like / their lives to be, and imagined / their strong, thick wings" (*DW* 68). Like the sheets of moss with their spiritual patience, and like the turtle with her blind wish, the crows, when they dream of what they would like to be, cannot imagine anything better than bursting into the sky on their "strong, thick wings." That makes them, says Oliver, perfect.

The poet is left, therefore, at a paradoxical impasse. Oliver desires, in Elder's words, "to subordinate her own projects to the reality around her, to enter into a world that baffles or even repels her, so that she can in turn bear witness to a reality beyond her concentric orders" (222). She perceives and admires the "perfection" in the nonhuman inhabiters of that reality, with their ability to remain content in the present moment. Yet she must acknowledge that she, in contrast, lacks such awareness and is thus separated from the rest of nature. She must necessarily remain, at least on some level, outside of that reality, unable to bear faithful witness.

It is not my intention to imply that this aspect of Oliver's work is somehow original or revolutionary. After all, Whitman's famous "I think I could turn and live with animals" passage from "Song of Myself" is only one of many famous articulations of the problem Oliver features here. However, Oliver's response to this impasse of both wanting to bear witness and recognizing the difficulty of doing so sets her apart from past thinkers—and many other ecopoets and nature writers as well—who have addressed this dilemma. Oliver's question, like those of Berry and Harjo and numerous others, is how to create place while also accepting and appreciating space; and like the poetry of her fellow ecopoets, most of Oliver's work can be read as an attempt to address this separation by realizing a relationship between herself and the natural world (hence to make place), while also remaining intellectually honest (and thus space-conscious) concerning the obstacles that impede that relationship. Yet within these similarities striking differences appear that demonstrate Oliver's heightened self-consciousness, which results in an even greater awareness of space than that displayed by Berry and Harjo.

OLIVER OFFERS a two-pronged response to the alienation resulting from the rift between humans and nature. The first prong, her poetics of the body, can be illuminated using the insights of phenomenology as presented by the philosopher David Abram, whose work descends directly from Edmund Husserl and Maurice Merleau-Ponty. Leonard Scigaj calls Merleau-Ponty's work "the most promising philosophical response for environmental literature to both poststructualism and to philosophical dualism, one that avoids solipsism and skepticism at the same time that it is very congenial to an ecological vision" (65). In its emphasis on the body as the central instrument of perception and on the relationship among the different bodies that make up what Husserl called an "intersubjective" world, phenomenology offers a useful lens through which to view the fundamentally phenomenological poetry of Oliver.

In *The Spell of the Sensuous* (1997), Abram echoes many contemporary theorists, beginning his discussion of the contemporary mindset with Descartes's division between the thinking mind and the material world, seen as leading to the development and domination of the experimental, objective sciences. The problem, according to Abram, is that "these sciences consistently overlook our ordinary, everyday experience of the world around us. Our direct experience is necessarily subjective, necessarily relative to our own position or place in the midst of things, to our particular desires, tastes, and concerns" (32):

> My life and the world's life are deeply intertwined; when I wake up one morning to find that a week-long illness has subsided and that my strength has returned, the world, when I step outside, fairly sparkles with energy and activity; waves of heat rise from the newly paved road smelling strongly of tar; the old red barn across the field juts into the sky at an intense angle. Likewise, when a haze descends upon the valley in which I dwell, it descends upon my awareness as well, muddling my thoughts, making my muscles yearn for sleep. The world and I reciprocate one another. The landscape as I directly experience it is hardly a determinate object; it is an ambiguous realm that responds to my emotions and calls forth feelings from me in turn. (33)

Therefore, contends Abram, to ignore this reciprocity and concentrate solely on "measurable" phenomena, rather than on the relationship between perceiver and perceived, is to limit oneself to a partial picture of reality.[1]

Phenomenology, in contrast, represents an attempt to explore the *interaction* between subject and object. Abram explains that phenomenology, as articulated by Husserl in the early twentieth century, "would turn toward 'the things themselves,' toward the world as it is experienced in its felt immediacy. Unlike the mathematics-based sciences, phenomenology would seek not to explain the world, but to describe as closely as possible the way the world makes itself evident to awareness, the way things first arise in our direct, sensorial experience" (35). As Pierre Thevenauz defines it, phenomenology is "neither a science of objects nor a science of subject; it is a science of *experience*. It does not concentrate exclusively on either the objects of experience or on the subject of experience, but on the point of contact where being and consciousness meet" (19).[2]

Working from the philosophy of Husserl and Merleau-Ponty, Abram asserts that this "point of contact where being and consciousness meet" is, at least from the perspective of the human perceiver, the body itself, "that mysterious and multifaceted phenomenon that seems always to accompany one's awareness, and indeed to be the very location of one's awareness within the field of appearances" (37). For it is solely the perceiving body and its five senses, Abram contends in a paraphrase of Merleau-Ponty, that makes us capable of experience:

> If this body is my very presence in the world, if it is the body that alone enables me to enter into relations with other presences, if without these eyes, this voice, or these hands I would be unable to see, to taste, and to touch things, or to be touched by them—if without this body, in other words, there would be no possibility of experience—then the body itself is the true subject of experience. (45)

Consequently, "the common notion of the experiencing self, or mind, as an immaterial phantom ultimately independent of the body can only be a mirage," for "at the heart of even our most abstract cogitations [lies] the sensuous and sentient life of the body itself" (45).

What keeps us from viewing ourselves as lone, isolated subjects, says Abram, is that our phenomenal field "also contains many *other* bodies, other forms that move and gesture in a fashion similar to one's own." This statement represents a crucial philosophical move, both for my argument and for Oliver's poetics of bodily identification, for Oliver largely avoids overemphasizing the self. As a result of what Husserl called an associative empathy, the "embodied subject comes to recognize these other bodies as other centers of experience, other subjects" (37). Thus the "field of appearances, while still a thoroughly subjective realm, [is] seen to be inhabited by *multiple* subjectivities; the phenomenal field [is] no longer the isolate haunt of a solitary ego, but a collective landscape, constituted by other experiencing subjects as well as by oneself" (37). And these subjects are not restricted to humans or even to humans and animals:

Each of us, in relation to the other, is both subject and object, sensible and sentient. Why, then, might this not also be the case in relation to another, nonhuman entity—a mountain lion, for instance, that I unexpectedly encounter in the northern forest? Indeed, such a meeting brings home to me even more forcefully that I am not just a sentient subject but also a sensible object, even an *edible* object, in the eyes (and nose) of the other. Even an ant crawling along my arm, visible to my eyes and tactile to my skin, displays at the same time its own sentience, responding immediately to my movements, even to the chemical changes of my mood. In relation to the ant I feel myself as a dense and material object, as capricious in my actions as the undulating earth itself. Finally, then, why might not this "reversibility" of subject and object extend to every entity that I experience? Once I acknowledge that my own sentience, or subjectivity, does not preclude my visible, tactile, objective existence for others, I find myself forced to acknowledge that *any* visible, tangible form that meets my gaze may also be an experiencing subject, sensitive and responsive to the beings around it, and to me. (67)

Consequently, "to the sensing body, *no* thing presents itself as utterly passive or inert" since, as a result of this reversibility of subject and object, the world around us is populated by other subjects (56). Instead, I and the world around me exist as part of an "ongoing reciprocity with the world" (56).

This intersubjective reciprocity—similar to the process Keith Basso calls "interanimation"—is central to Oliver's poetry of the body. Often, in fact, the poet's body and that of the world are depicted as being so interrelated that they easily become confused with one another. In the title poem from *West Wind*, for instance, Oliver speaks of listening to night birds singing in a garden and then writes, "Oh, listen! / For a moment I thought it was / our own bodies" (48). As Abram explains, this "ambiguity of experience is already a part of any phenomenon that draws our attention. For whatever we perceive is necessarily entwined with our own subjectivity, already blended with the dynamism of life and sentience" (34). We see this pattern repeatedly in Oliver's work, as in "White Flowers," where the speaker tells of feeling "near / that porous line / where my own body was done with / and the roots and the stems and the flowers / began" (*NS* 58). And in "Am I Not among the Early Risers" she writes of the bond that exists between her own body and that of the earth:

> Here is an amazement—once I was twenty years old and in
>   every motion of my body there was a delicious ease,
>   and in every motion of the green earth there was
>   a hint of paradise,
>   and now I am sixty years old, and it is the same. (*WW* 7)

Inherent within Oliver's delight concerning the "porous line" that divides her from the rest of the transhuman world is a longing to recognize and consciously experience a reciprocal and intimate relationship with nature, "the old river that runs through everything" (*PH* 106).

This intimacy arises from Oliver's poetics of the body. The poet Vicki Graham explains that "over and over the speaker of Oliver's poems reminds herself to look, to touch, to taste, to see, and to smell. Only by yielding to her senses can she get close to the 'real'" (355). In both of her recent prose handbooks on poetry, Oliver discusses this idea, spelling out her understanding of the relationship between nature and the body and sounding a great deal like Merleau-Ponty:

> We experience the physical world around us through our five senses. Through our imagination and our intelligence, we recall, organize, conceptualize, and meditate. What we meditate upon is never shapeless or filled with alien emotion—it is filled with all the precise earthly things that we have ever encountered and all of our responses to them. The task of the meditation is to put disorder into order. No one could think, without first living among living things. No one would need to think, without the initial profusion of perceptual experience. (*PH* 105)

As Oliver proceeds from this phenomenological assertion, she explains that poetry evolves directly out of the relationship between nature and the body:

> The natural world has always been the great warehouse of symbolic imagery. Poetry is one of the ancient arts, and it began, as did all the fine arts, within the original wilderness of the earth. Also, it began through

the process of seeing, and feeling, and hearing, and smelling, and touching, and then remembering—I mean *remembering in words*—what these perceptual experiences were like, while trying to describe the endless invisible fears and desire of our inner lives. The poet used the actual, known event or experience to elucidate the inner, invisible experience—or, in other words, the poet used figurative language, relying for those figures on the natural world. (*PH* 106)

Consequently, Oliver maintains, "the reader without perceptual experience with the natural processes is locked out of the poetry of our world," because there is such an intense relationship between poetry, the world, and the body (*PH* 107).

Through an act of imaginative reunification, Oliver uses her poetry to insert her body into the body of the world. As Janet McNew explains, Oliver's poetry often produces "the opposite of transcendence" as it aims at highlighting the linkage between the body and the earth (62). In the words of Judith Kitchen, "Everywhere [Oliver] exhibits an impulse toward fusion, toward discovering a place where the speaker can lay down her human burden and, quite literally, become one with the natural order" (150). Consider, for instance, the closing lines from "Ghosts," in which Oliver renders a dream of witnessing a buffalo cow giving birth to and then nursing its newborn calf. After describing the intimate moment the speaker says, "And I asked them, / in my dream I knelt down and asked them / to make room for me" ("Ghosts" *AP* 30). We see here the poet's recognition of her separateness, as well as her desire to overcome it by, in essence, allowing her body to *become* an animal, in this case a buffalo calf.

Her poem "The Sea" takes this concept of interconnection as its central theme, set up visually in the poem's opening lines, lapping like the ocean surf itself, that narrate the speaker's desire to return, while swimming in the sea, to a state of natural "perfection":

Stroke by
    stroke my
        body remembers that life and cries for
            the lost parts of itself—
fins, gills

opening like flowers into
  the flesh—my legs
   want to lock and become
one muscle, I swear I know
  just what the blue-gray scales
   shingling
    the rest of me would
feel like!

Recalling Harjo's work, the poem suggests that memory offers the possibility for recovering a relationship with the world in which the swimmer is immersed, for "a spillage / of nostalgia pleads / from the very bones!" The poem concludes by describing the body's desire to return to its natural origin. Oliver writes that her bones "long to give up the long trek / inland, the brittle / beauty of understanding, / and dive," so that she becomes "a flaming body / of blind feeling" and achieves a union with the sea itself (69–70). In this longing we see Oliver's (admittedly impossible) desire to identify so intensely with her body that she overcomes her hyperrational self and attains something like the perfection of animals.[3]

As Abram explains, a bodily identification with the nonhuman world offers us the means for the (at least temporary) reconnection that Oliver seeks. According to Abram, much of our perceived isolation results from our inherited worldview grounded in the great chain of being—"the hierarchical ordering that locates 'humans,' by virtue of our incorporeal intellect, above and apart from all other, 'merely corporeal,' entities" (48).[4] "Such hierarchies," Abram says, "are wrecked by any phenomenology that takes seriously our immediate sensory experience. For our senses disclose to us a wild-flowering proliferation of entities and elements, in which humans are thoroughly immersed. While this diversity of sensuous forms certainly displays some sort of reckless order, we find ourselves in the midst of, rather than on top of, this order" (48–49). Thus, "the body is precisely my insertion in the common, or intersubjective, field of experience" (44):

The breathing, sensing body draws its sustenance and its very substance from the soils, plants, and elements that surround it; it continually contributes itself, in turn, to the air, to the composing earth, to the nourishment of insects and oak trees and squirrels, ceaselessly spreading out of itself as well as breathing the world into itself, so that it is very difficult to discern, at any moment, precisely where this living body begins and where it ends. . . . Ultimately, to acknowledge the life of the body, and to affirm our solidarity with this physical form, is to acknowledge our existence as one of earth's animals, and so to remember and rejuvenate the organic basis of our thoughts and our intelligence. (46–47)

Again, Abram and Oliver echo each other. Abram's observation that "it is very difficult to discern, at any moment, precisely where this living body begins and where it ends" sounds strikingly similar to Oliver's many lyrics celebrating the porous line separating her body from that of the nonhuman natural world.[5]

Moreover, Abram's phenomenological explanation of the body's relationship with the nonhuman natural world illustrates a fundamental of Oliver's poetics. In her emphasis on recognizing the body as the connecting phenomenon uniting human and nonhuman physical forms, in her affirmation of "our solidarity with this physical form," Oliver moves to a phenomenological acknowledgment of the biological, and thus natural, relationship between humans and nonhumans. To return to Tuanian terminology, this relational solidarity offers the means to view the world as a place, allowing humans the opportunity to feel connected to, and at home in, the natural world. This insight does not, of course, completely restore the "broken connection" Oliver continually returns to, but it does balance it by emphasizing that the rift we create through our language and logic is only part of the picture, a picture that allows for a recognition of both division and relationship.

TO SUMMARIZE, Oliver's poetry displays a keen awareness of the modern divorce, produced largely as a result of human logic and rationality, between humans and the rest of the natural world. The first component of her two-pronged response to this dualistic split is an attempt to view the world phenomenologically, by recognizing the essential relationship between her own body and the rest of nature. Oliver's poetry works from the assumption that, in the words of Neil Evernden, "once we accept, through the study of Nature, that all life is organically related, organically the same through the linkage of evolution, then humanity is literally a part of Nature. Not figuratively, not poetically, but literally an object like other natural objects" (*Creation* 93). This place-conscious awareness of humanity's organic relationship with nonhuman nature coexists with and balances, in Oliver's work, her space-conscious cognizance of her own estrangement from the natural world. It calls for both a Berry-like observation of and commitment to natural subjects around us and a Harjo-like willingness to adjust our perspectives on the natural world.

As a transition to the second prong of Oliver's response to this estrangement, her use of the pathetic fallacy, consider the final section of "The Gardens," the concluding poem of *American Primitive* (1983). In this poem, reminiscent of Berry's "To the Unseeable Animal," Oliver enters a garden, where her body comes into contact with the body of the whole of nature, to which she addresses her questions regarding how she could ever come to know its fullness. She then continues:

You gleam
as you lie back
breathing like something
taken from water,
a sea creature, except
for your two human legs
which tremble
and open
into the dark country
I keep dreaming of. How
shall I touch you
unless it is
everywhere?
I begin here and there,
finding you,
the heart within you,
and the animal,
and the voice; I ask

over and over
for your whereabouts, trekking
wherever you take me,
the boughs of your body
leading deeper into the trees,
over the white fields,
the rivers of bone,
the shouting,
the answering, the rousing,
great run toward the interior,
the unseen, the unknowable
center. (86–87)

Here the human speaker enters the wild and foreign nonhuman world and, through her recognition of a biological kinship to that world (with its "two human legs"), merges with the whole of nature to the extent that the speaker and her world are barely distinguishable. One can still make the distinction at the poem's conclusion, however, for at that point the speaker is still narrating her journey toward "the interior."[6] Graham suggests that the speaker ultimately does merge with the natural world she describes, arguing that since the poem concludes the collection, "the blank space at the end of 'The Gardens' implies that Oliver has lost herself in the 'body of another'" (366). While I agree with the essence of Graham's reading of the poem's conclusion, I would amend it slightly by pointing out that the lyric ends with a reference not to "the center" into which we can assume the speaker coalesces, but to "the *unknowable* center." My sense of the poem is that the speaker narrates her "great run *toward* the interior," but that she concludes the poem (and the collection) with an admission that while her body allows her to experience a very real and fundamental connection between herself and her world, that center is ultimately "unknowable."[7] As such, the poem is both place- and space-conscious, offering a vision of a world in which humans can feel at home yet never fully comprehend or join.

These observations are also relevant to Oliver's two distinct but complementary uses of the pathetic fallacy and its chief vehicle, personification. Oliver repeatedly personifies her nonhuman subjects in her attempts to convey her own experiences, again and again referring to their emotions, their desires, and even their philosophical musings. She speaks of an owl turning its face from the poet "in disgust" (*NS* 23); of the sea "divid[ing] / with perfect courtesy, to let you in" (*WW* 61); of the sun "rising, / scrap[ing] his orange breast / on the thick pines" (*WW* 41); of the ocean "empty[ing] its pockets— / foam and fluff" (*WW* 29). Oliver discusses the reason for these repeated personifications in *Rules for the Dance*, where she explains that personification can "create an intimacy" between writer and inanimate object. It can create "a sense, however impossible logically, of an operating will" (71). Notice, however, Oliver's recognition that personification can create only "a sense" of an operating will, and that actually understanding the workings of the Other's mind is "impossible logically"; in other words, because of the lack of mutuality, it is practically impossible to say with any certainty that such an intimacy could occur. With this admission, Oliver emphasizes the problems surrounding the device and demonstrates that her use of it is not unconscious but intentional.[8]

The fact that Oliver personifies is less interesting than the question of *how* she handles the pathetic fallacy, for it is here that she distinguishes herself from many other ecopoets. Often, she steadfastly refuses to enter another subject's consciousness at all. Think, for instance, of her poem "The Shark," narrated from the perspective of the fish "hunters," in which she carefully describes the landing of a shark from outside the fish's perspective, never venturing into its thoughts and emotions via the pathetic fallacy. We see the entire struggle from the viewpoint of the fishers. But as her career has evolved, Oliver has increasingly played what she calls the "imaginer" role, choosing not to remain outside of her subjects' consciousness and instead actually speaking for the animate and even inanimate natural elements she describes. In examining her tendency to grant natural entities not only sentience but also emotions and intellectual and spiritual insight, it becomes apparent that Oliver utilizes two distinct versions of the pathetic fallacy, one that personifies self-reflexively, and one that does so with no hint of apology for speaking for an other. The manner in which she speaks for her subjects and the amount of self-conscious awareness she demonstrates in doing so reveal a great deal about Oliver's poetics and philosophy.

For example, in the above lines from "Landscape," Oliver employs two important words as she observes the early-morning crows and speculates on the birds' state of mind. She writes that they "burst up into the sky — *as though* / all night they had thought of what they would like / their lives to be, and imagined / their strong, thick wings" (*DW* 68, emphasis added). The phrase — "as though" — and other similar ones ("as if," "I think," "if," "it seems") appear throughout Oliver's poetry and represent rhetorically ethical gestures that acknowledge that the poet is appropriating nature for her own ends; in these gestures Oliver emphasizes her awareness of the danger of assuming that we can actually communicate, or even understand, the consciousness of animals and other forms of wildlife.

Such examples pervade her work, as when the word "if" repeatedly appears in "West Wind": the poet says that "the speck of my heart" sings out, "the way the sun would sing if the sun could sing, if light had a mouth and a tongue, if the sky had a throat" (*WW* 47). And in "Her Grave," Oliver points to different examples of nonhuman nature as models of humility and gratitude, but in doing so she highlights the fact that she is imposing her own ruminations and values on the subjects of the poem:

> Does the hummingbird think he himself invented his crimson throat?
> He is wiser than that, *I think.*
>   [......................]
> Do the cranes crying out in the high clouds
> think it is all their own music?
>   [......................]
> Does the bear wandering in the autumn up the side of the hill
> think all by herself she has imagined the refuge and the refreshment
> of her long slumber? (*NS* 15, emphasis added)

Notice here the different levels at which Oliver makes her point. With the phrase "I think" she acknowledges her own inability to discern with any certainty the hummingbird's wisdom or the bear's imaginings. At the same time, the lines — focusing on the singers' throats, music, and imaginings — point to the vocation of the poet, to whose imaginative song we listen as we read the poem. Thus the lines become a form of warning to the speaker herself and to fellow poets, cautioning against poetic hubris. The following lines reinforce the admonition and widen its audience: "A dog can never tell you what she knows from the / smells of the world, but you know, watching her, that you know / almost nothing." Again, Oliver acknowledges her essential ignorance when it comes to understanding the nonhuman world.

We see her taking a similar approach in the opening stanzas of "Have You Ever Tried to Enter the Long Black Branches":

Have you ever tried to enter the long black branches
    of other lives—
tried to imagine what the crisp fringes, full of honey,
    hanging
from the branches of the young locust trees, in early summer,
    feel like?

Do you think this world is only an entertainment for you?

Never to enter the sea and notice how the water divides
    with perfect courtesy, to let you in!
Never to lie down on the grass, as though you were the grass!
Never to leap to the air as you open your wings over
    the dark acorn of your heart!

No wonder we hear, in your mournful voice, the complaint
    that something is missing from your life! (*WW* 61)

Again, in words like "tried," "imagine," and "as though," a self-conscious awareness appears as Oliver emphasizes both her desire to identify with the branches, the grass, and the birds, and the importance of acknowledging our essential inability to enter their minds and experiences. The explicit message here is that the decision "never to enter the long black branches / of other lives" carries with it consequences, in this case a sensation of isolation and incompleteness. The poem also implies that even an imagined integration into nature is better than none at all.

Yet while Oliver often self-reflexively highlights the logical impossibility of understanding the consciousness of nonhuman subjects, she just as often neglects to do so and presents an unapologetic and even celebratory rendering of, say, an animal's dreams or a flower's emotional state. In other words, her verse at times exemplifies the point Michael J. McDowell makes when, discussing Fromm and the illusion of objectivity, he argues that we are beginning to see the pathetic fallacy as "not merely a Romantic indulgence, but [as] an inevitable component of human perception; it is something to acknowledge and celebrate, not to condemn" (373). In fact, Oliver frequently moves back and forth, one moment unselfconsciously depicting her subject's feelings or desires, the next moment employing the self-reflexive "as though" strategy.

A representative example of this oscillating effect can be seen in "Maples," from *West Wind* (1997). This lyric, which describes "happy" trees that enjoy the rain and having their feet chained to the ground, abounds with the use of the pathetic fallacy. Yet in typical Oliver fashion, almost hidden in the center of the poem lies an explicit statement of her awareness of the problematic nature of her description: "nobody can prove it but any fool can feel it." The complexity of this clause should not be overlooked. After offering a litany of phrases that many contemporary readers would consider a naïve throwback to a now-extinct, overly romantic nature poetry, Oliver acknowledges that the experience she renders cannot be logically "proven." However, without starting a new sentence or even breaking the line, Oliver counteracts that rationality, in effect trumping it with what she obviously believes to be a transcendent force: feeling. What Oliver describes here, as she does in so many of her other poems, is an intense bodily, emotive, and intellectual experience that takes place between herself and others who populate her intersubjective world. Oliver understands the dicey proposition she underwrites when she ascribes emotions to the maples, yet she takes the risk rather than forfeit her desire to translate the experience.[9]

We see this same concept in "This Morning Again It Was in the Dusty Pines" in its incorporation of different types of personification. Like "Maples," this poem begins in a mode of unselfconscious personification, with the poet ascribing emotions (shyness, disgust) to an owl, emotions to which the speaker could, of course, have no access. But as the owl flies from her sight and she imagines its disdain for its observer—presumably for the poet's own frailties and weaknesses—the poet inserts a parenthetical question concerning the absence of communication between herself and the bird. As she wonders what message she might impart to the "perfect" bird if she had the means and a common language, the speaker realizes that she would have nothing of value (to the owl) to say. Consequentially, the tone of the poem's personification shifts here, as the poet catalogues responses that would *not* be appropriate—admonition, blame, worship—then highlights the fact that any true understanding between the two subjects takes place only in the "as-though" realm, within a conversation "you must imagine." In response to her admission that even as a poet she "cannot improve upon the scene" but must remain in "stony silence," the speaker concludes the poem by retreating from personification and simply offering an observation, albeit a poetic one, of the flight of the owl (*NS* 23).

This technique of Oliver's, what John Elder calls "her characteristic shuttle of observation and sympathy," is closely related to her phenomenological worldview; it is because of her bodily identification with nonhuman nature that Oliver finds it necessary to move among these different perspectives, to shift from one side of the water to the other (Elder 223). For since she views those with whom she comes into contact as relatives in an intersubjective world, it follows that she would desire both to experience that kinship by imagining their thoughts and emotions while also respecting and acknowledging those subjects' ultimate autonomy, including their ownership of their own minds and emotions. (As Merwin interprets Blake, "One both can be and can never be the bird.") In creating intimacy between herself and nonhuman nature, she makes place; in recognizing its logical impossibility, she acknowledges the spatial nature of the world.

In this place- and space-consciousness Oliver echoes Berry and Harjo, while also taking a step further in her awareness of the space side of the binary. Oliver's ability to remain self-conscious concerning the dubiousness of her own intimacy with nature represents an additional bow toward space-consciousness. She longs for connection no less than the other ecopoets, yet is more direct in her acknowledgment of the impossibility of her quest. While Berry and Harjo are certainly not naïvely optimistic in their belief that we can easily "go back" and find a way to reconnect with the natural world, their verse is much less self-conscious than Oliver's when it comes to demonstrating an awareness of the fallibility of its attempts at reunification with nature.

I WANT TO RETURN now to Tuan, who, like other contemporary theorists, asserts that the rift between human and nonhuman nature produces other intraspecies consequences for modern people, who become "islanded" selves divorced not only from an indifferent natural world but from the rest of humanity as well. For Tuan, place, along with culture, offers a feeling of connection to the world and thus the means to "forget our separateness and the world's indifference" (*Two Essays* 44); but it does so only through delusion, in that no matter how strongly we feel related to an other, that feeling is, to a significant extent, illusory. So for Tuan, the only reasonable response to the modern crisis is to "acknowledge the realty of 'islanded' selves and the world's indifference, peer 'beyond' the carapaces of place and culture in all their myriad enthralling forms, and, by thus putting a slight distance between us and what we create, recognize not only their necessity and power to delude but also their goodness and beauty" (*Two Essays* 45–46). Tuan advocates that we accept modern alienation as fact; that we recognize the delusional nature of place and culture; and that we acknowledge both the "necessity and power" and the "goodness and beauty" of those delusions in helping us to deal with the perceived rift between people and nature.

The response Tuan endorses mirrors that of Oliver, whose work at its best weaves in and out among several philosophical perspectives. Unlike many traditional nature poets, she embraces the fact that the world is indifferent, and that in many ways, primarily as a consequence of her human logic and rationality, hers is an "islanded" self. Yet at the same time she realizes that the material and biological essence of her body serves as a significant point of relation between herself and the Others surrounding her. This awareness of relatedness leads to place-making, as Oliver uses her personifying poetry to enter the world of the nonhuman subjects around her; she also invites them to enter her own, thus imagining a place-full world that serves as home for humans and nonhumans alike. Yet she tempers attempts at connection with a space-conscious awareness of her essential inability to achieve either goal; the chasm between herself and nonhuman nature is wide. She never loses sight of the fact that the product of this poetic place-making is ultimately a mere "carapace"—"a protective, decorative, or disguising shell"[10]—in its "myriad enthralling forms," which she has created in order to impose a sense of connection between herself and those about whom she writes. But still, she is able to see in her impositions "not only their necessity and power to delude but also their goodness and beauty."

This pervasive intermingling of seemingly mutually exclusive perspectives lends great power to Oliver's work. As she says of herself, "This is my skill—I am capable of pondering the most detailed knowledge, and the most fastened-up, impenetrable mystery, at the same time" (*WW* 16). Her "skill" is in making place by "creating an intimacy" that links her with those around her, while simultaneously affirming and embracing space in her acknowledgment of the "logical impossibility" of an absolute and unbroken intimacy.

CHAPTER FIVE

Between the Earth and Silence

W. S. Merwin

now I find myself wishing
to be here to be alive here
it is impossible enough to still be the wish of a child

—W. S. Merwin, "Waves in August"

IN HIS SHORT 1992 poem "Utterance," W. S. Merwin writes of sitting "over words" and hearing a sound, "a kind of whispered sighing," that transcends language. This sound exists somewhere beyond the earth and the poet's ability to convey it, but still not in the realm of silence where it cannot be heard—it is "spinning its one syllable / between the earth and silence" (*RIT* 44). Merwin's dilemma is to communicate his experience with the unarticulable sound that has so moved him, while still honoring its ultimate unattainability. From his earliest work, Merwin has repeatedly explored this tension, attempting to address issues of consequence while highlighting the ineptitude of the very language he employs. Merwin demonstrates, in the words of Leonard Scigaj, an awareness that, although "language cannot capture the essences in the referential world," the poet can still actively search "for an originary language that tries to close the gap between words and intense, firsthand experience in that referential world" (41). Like many other ecopoets, Merwin has, throughout his diverse and continually evolving career, dealt with this conflict by offering a vision of the world that values the interaction between place and space. But whereas ecopoets like Berry, Harjo, and Oliver find a way to blend these two concepts in their work, Merwin's poetry displays a consistent unease when it comes to finding this balance. Because of his skepticism concerning human language and its ability to communicate something meaningful about the world, Merwin often displays a reluctance toward offering finalizing statements, even about matters for which he feels intensely passionate. Instead, his poetry tends toward silence.

LIKE THE OTHER ecopoets discussed here, Merwin depicts the world as a community founded on reciprocity between human and nonhuman nature. As he explained to me in a 1998 interview, "I think that it's a great delusion to feel that we are separate from the world. I mean, what we see on the outside and what we are on the inside, we can't tell where the one starts and the other one goes on, and if we damage one we damage the other. We can't make that separation" ("'This *Absolutely* Matters'" 1–2). Much of his poetry, he said, arises out of an "ability to imagine the circumstances and suffering and predicaments of other lives and of other kinds of lives, and indeed of the whole of life":

And I believe that if you come to a sympathy in your life, an individual one or generically in regard to a species or the whole of life, you can't pull back from it. Once your sympathy expands to a certain point, you can't shrink the horizon again. If you do, you begin to sort of atrophy. I think if it's that important, you can't sort of push it out of your mind, which means you can't push it out of your thoughts and imagination and you wake up some time in the middle of the night and it's bothering you. And then you find that it's entering into the way language occurs and the way you're hearing it. That's, to me, where poetry begins. It's not with ideas, and it's not with principles, and it's not with platforms. It's hearing something in language, and seeing where that language goes by itself. (3–4)

Thus for Merwin, thought, imagination, language, and poetry all emerge out of what he calls a sympathy for "other lives and of other kinds of lives." In other words, his poetics issue forth out of his desire to grant subjectivity to (both human and nonhuman) others. This willingness to view the world intersubjectively leads to the type of place-making commitment Merwin has made to protecting nonhuman nature, for instance in the rainforest he is currently working to restore near his Hawaiian home.

Throughout his career, Merwin has looked to articulate this relationship with the world around him, as in "Burning Mountain" from *The Drunk in the Furnace* (1960), in which he personifies a mountain, highlighting its mutual bond with the humans around it and emphasizing its "heart" and "veins" (*FFB* 254–255).[1] Likewise, in a poem from *Rain in the Trees* (1988), he writes, "By the tree touching the tree I hear the tree / I walk with the tree / we talk" (7). Merwin asserts that the earth "is still a very beautiful place; it's seldom enough that it's seen [in and of itself]. It's seen as an object of exploitation, rather than as something of which we are a part. We are neither superior nor inferior, we are a part of it. It is not different from us. So when we treat it with contempt and we exploit it, we are despising ourselves" ("W. S. Merwin: An Interview" 22). This attitude demonstrates the essence of a Tuanian sense of place, one that assigns a high priority to viewing the world as a community connected in a symbiotic web.

It follows, then, that Merwin's awareness of the reciprocal relationship between himself and a more-than-human world would result in a deep attachment to that world. Jane Frazier writes that "like Thoreau, what Merwin strives for in many of his nature poems is contact with a lost, original world, free from the ontologically insular and physically threatening forces of industrialization and technology—a condition in which humans exist in community with their surroundings" (16). His lyrics consistently return to this affection. Notice, for example, the attention to details and the appreciation of place in "Sheep Passing," from Merwin's 1999 *The River Sound*, where the poet images "mayflies hover[ing] throughout the lone evening" and tells of a winding lane in which "the stream of sheep runs among shadows calling / the old throats gargling again uphill / along known places once more and from the bells / borne by their predecessors." The music from these bells is "dull as wood" and "clonk[s] to the flutter of all / the small hooves over the worn stone" (120). In Tuanian terms, this description—of the lane, the sheep, the hooves, the worn stone, the sound of the bells worn by generation after generation of sheep—is not "a confusion of images" to a new resident, but a significant *place* endowed with value by one familiar with the neighborhood.

Especially in *The River Sound* (1999), a collection largely devoted to the past, Merwin expresses a nostalgia about his former place(s). The centerpiece of the collection, the long poem "Testimony," focuses particularly on this affinity for place. Speaking to his wife, Paula, for instance, about their experiences with the land around them, Merwin describes the two of them listening to "the long notes of those nightingales" "as we lie watching the moonlight / that has remembered everything / the stones of the old house shining / the cloud of light veiling the hill / and the river below shining upwards as though it were still" (88).

Just as often, though, we see the flip side of this issue, as Merwin's poetry, much like that of Harjo, laments the "placelessness" of modern society, whose members often seem completely unaware of the bond between themselves and the rest of the world. One of the best examples appears in "Native Trees," which begins with the lines "Neither my father nor my mother knew / the names of the trees / where I was born." The poet tells of asking, as a boy, the names of the trees around him, but his parents failed even to look where he pointed. The lyric concludes in the voice of the child, asking whether trees existed where his parents were children, and whether they had seen them. The parents' answer typifies the placelessness Merwin condemns, for the boy knows that "when they said yes it meant / they did not remember." The child asks the names of those trees, "but both my father and my mother / said they never knew" (*RIT* 6). The fact that they cannot name each species or individual tree is not, of course, the issue for Merwin. Rather, it is the lack of attention to and awareness of the more-than-human world around us that he laments.

He takes up the issue of placelessness again, albeit less subtly, in "Airport." In this poem the airport is described as being "devoted to absence in life," in that "the building is not inhabited it is not / home except to roaches / it is not loved it is serviced"; the airport "is not a place / but a container with signs / directing a process." Then, after describing the building, the poet turns to its consumers and, in first person, concludes by saying, "We travel far and fast / and as we pass through we forget / where we have been" (*RIT* 55). The implication, again in accord with Harjo, is clear: by delivering ourselves up to such a placeless lifestyle, we lose a sense of ourselves, as well as an awareness of our past, of "where we have been," and thus of who we are.

Consequently, then, this placelessness can lead to a lack of connection to the nonhuman world. Some of Merwin's best-known poems deal with the disappearance of species that results from this lack of place-awareness, like the shorebirds he refers to which, "while I think of them . . . are growing rare" (*RS* 124). The opening lines of "Orioles" underscore the same issue: "The song of the oriole began as an echo / but this year it was not heard afterward" (*RS* 117). And as he points out in "The Asians Dying," the exploitation and destruction of parts of the nonhuman world offer serious consequences for the human world as well, for "when the forests have been destroyed their darkness remains" (*SFB* 118). Frazier notes that for Merwin, "the epistemological and physical distance between ourselves and nature that we have increasingly created has divided us from our most important psychic resource and the basis of our being. Humans are a part of a collective universe, and by shaping the world to accommodate our immediate desires we have gone far to eliminate the original conditions that we need for a complete, healthy environment" (41). Much of Merwin's poetry works from the assumption that a commitment to place helps prevent physical and psychological disasters, whereas placelessness has the potential to produce them.

LIKE BERRY, Harjo, and Oliver, Merwin makes the process of place-making a central theme in his poetry. Much of the time, however, that process is overshadowed by a space-conscious awareness of the limitations of human insight, language, and even poetry itself. This ever-present space-consciousness, perhaps the most prominent characteristic of Merwin's work and much different from placelessness, is based on an alert, fundamental humility regarding what we can and cannot know, can and cannot control. Thus we see, in "The Comet Museum" from Merwin's 2001 *The Pupil*, a description of the comet as a phenomenon that existed in a moment that is "beyond reckoning // beyond time beyond memory"; even photos of the comet are merely "pictures that someone took / of what escaped us" (4). And as in the work of the other ecopoets, Merwin's space-consciousness emerges out of a mindful relationship with place, since a deep knowledge of place produces a respectful awareness of our own limitations.

For example, dominating *The River Sound* is the concept that the world is older than our names for it. The collection repeatedly declares that our experiences with the world are negligible in comparison with the world itself, and that the names we offer in trying to communicate that world are hopelessly inadequate. Merwin's speakers refer to stones falling away "as they had / been falling before I had ever seen them" (121), and to "sounds from before there were voices" (9).[2] Often, Merwin stresses the earth and its nonhuman inhabitants' longevity in contrast to that of humankind. In "The Garden of Versailles," for instance, he distinguishes the longevity of the flora and the river from "the king whom / they called The Sun in his day [who] is nobody again" (*RS* 8).

The conclusion of "To the Insects" offers the same recognition—paralleling Berry and Oliver—that humans will literally enter and become part of the earth after death. But Merwin diverges slightly from Berry's and Oliver's handling of this theme by taking the next step, foreseeing not only the individual's joining with the insects under the earth, but the disappearance of the human species as a whole. We hear in the poem not only the condemnation of humanity's suicidal tendency to exhaust the "earth and the water," but also the poet's space-conscious awareness that the world is greater than and outlasts humanity, which is a mere part of nature (*RIT* 49).

For Merwin, this humble awareness of Tuanian space results in a prizing of ignorance, which represents the path to wisdom. He makes this case in his interview with Folsom and Nelson, where he refers to Thoreau's essay "Walking" and argues that

> a real poem comes out of what you don't know. You write it with what you know, but finally its source is what you don't know. There's a passage where Thoreau says, "How can someone find his ignorance if he has to use his knowledge all the time?" The arrogance would be the assumption that what you know has some kind of final value and you can depend on it, and it will get rid of a whole world which you will never know, which really informs it. (335–336)

This appreciation of ignorance results in lines where Merwin speaks of "the beam of some / star familiar but in no sense known," or where he hears the song of a wren but is careful to point out that he hears it "without understanding" ("The Wren" *RS* 114).

The theme of humble ignorance also emerges in Merwin's poem "February," when those he refers to as "the dead" deliver a message from the grave, pronouncing, "I know nothing / learn from me" (*SFB* 168). In "Provision" the speaker says, "I will take with me the emptiness of my hands / What you do not have you find everywhere" (*SFB* 113). Here ignorance is exalted over conventional knowledge, which is usually connected with the *acquisition* of wisdom. Instead, the image of the empty hands suggests that it is precisely the humility of ignorance that provides the opportunity for true understanding.

"The Saint of the Uplands" also takes ignorance as its primary theme. The speaker of this poem, the saint himself, tries to make clear to his followers that the ignorance of humanity is a gift to be appreciated. He states that his supporters' devotion to and reliance on him have actually cost them an understanding of themselves, explaining to the reader, "I gave them / Nothing but what was theirs." He describes the people's eyes as "empty"

and says that for them, vision "might not come otherwise / Than as water."
He then metonymically links this vision-bringing water with ignorance and
mystery, as he tells of teaching the people that they have their own streams
of water, their own ignorance:

> I took a single twig from the tree of my ignorance
> And divined the living streams under
> Their very houses. I showed them
> The same tree growing in their dooryards.
> You have ignorance of your own, I said.
> They have ignorance of their own.

Here, New Testament language such as "living streams" suggests a theme of
redemption. With tree images calling to mind both the tree of knowledge of
good and evil and the Crucifixion, and vision being "divined" from under
these trees of ignorance, the saint implies that the ignorance that brings vi-
sion, understanding, and redemption comes as a result of acknowledging the
mystery that exists within everyone.

The poem concludes with the saint despondent over his inability to in-
struct the people in any meaningful way at all.

> I taught them nothing.
> Everywhere
> The eyes are returning under the stones. And over
> My dry bones they build their churches, like wells. (*SFB* 20).

Instead of understanding the ignorant vision the saint speaks of, the fol-
lowers forsake their own streams of ignorance and instead build churches
over the "dry bones" of the dead teacher. In their efforts to understand the
religion and achieve salvation, the people have actually lost their own truth.
By searching for the light, they have missed the meaning in the darkness.

Related to the concept of healthy ignorance is the notion of letting go of
the need to "understand," to "reason out," a world that often transcends rea-
son. In "Lackawanna," from *The Carrier of Ladders* (1971), the speaker nar-
rates the process of attempting to understand the river, which by the end of
the poem will represent salvation. The speaker addresses the river, explain-
ing that originally it signified fear for him; he describes it as the "black"

river "rising dark," calling himself the "obedient child" who "shrank from you." He says, "I ran / told to be afraid / obedient." As the poem continues, the narrator tells of his maturation, yet the fear remains; as he explains to the river, "Through the night the dead drifted down you / all the dead / what was found later no one could recognize."

Then suddenly the narrator "wakes up" in the present moment, and he finds himself already standing in the frightening river:

I wake black to the knees
so it has happened
I have set foot in you
both feet
Jordan
too long I was ashamed
at a distance (*SFB* 163–164)

Here the rational, objective logic of the narrator has lost its power over him, and the result is salvation. The adults had counseled him to avoid the frightening river, as had his logical mind. Yet when, in his sleep, he steps into the shadows of the water, he discovers that he is standing in the baptismal waters of the Jordan.

In "The Lantern," from *Writings to an Unfinished Accompaniment* (1973), Merwin makes the same point, imagining a place where reason-based opposites do not exist, thus allowing the dwellers there to comprehend the oneness of creation. When you see this world, Merwin says, "you are there already," because "in that world nothing can break / so no one believes in the plural there" and, therefore, "at last there is only / the single / one / alone / held together by nothing / so the question of belief never arises." This place where "no one believes in the plural" is "the place of a god," because here the dualities that create faith and doubt do not exist (*SFB* 275). Mark Christhilf explains that "in Merwin's story the great sin is division—an act in which mankind separates things from the fabric of being and subjects them to particular uses. Division is for Merwin a category of human reason. It is the tendency to compare, contrast, and define, and it causes humankind to live in the historical realm, which is fallen, jaded, copied" (49).

Thus, in "Is That What You Are," dualities maim those who depend on them. In this lyric, the speaker addresses a "new ghost," who has died so recently that he or she is still standing among the living, who are called "the unfinished." The speaker, one of the unfinished, explains that "hope and grief are still our wings" and that these are "why we cannot fly" (*SFB* 81). The implication is that the living humans are bound to their mortality and consequently still view life according to apparent dichotomies, in this case hope and grief. In response, Merwin calls his readers to a realm in which they can transcend apparent opposites and recognize the unity that exists in all of life.

Merwin's work continually returns to this theme, reminding its readers to value ignorance and recognize that experience cannot be captured or "understood," even by the poet. The Heraclitus quotation Merwin chose as the epigraph to *The Lice* (1967) is a prime example:

> All men are deceived by the appearances of things, even Homer himself, who was the wisest man in Greece; for he was deceived by boys catching lice: they said to him, "What we have caught and what we have killed we have left behind, but what has escaped us we bring with us."

In his reading of this passage, Thomas B. Byers says that the epigraph sets up "a poetics not of self, but of self-restraint." For Merwin, writes Byers, "poems must not consent to the catching and killing of final statement or formal closure. Rather, they must 'escape' authority—go beyond the poet's largely delusive powers to fix and order—if they are to accompany the self on its journey" (81). Allowing the subjects of his poems—for Merwin, both human and nonhuman nature—to "escape authority," is a fundamentally space-conscious act. He stressed this idea in a 1983 interview:

> I think that poetry, and maybe all writing, certainly everything we do to some degree, does not come out of what you know, but out of what you don't know. And one of the great superficialities of positivistic thinking is the assumption that things really evolve out of what you know. Nothing evolves out of what you know. You don't move from what you know to something else you know. And it's the unknown that keeps rendering possibilities. ("Possibilities of the Unknown" 168)

To accept that the unknown renders possibilities is to practice the appreciation of Tuanian space.

AS I'VE DEMONSTRATED in earlier chapters, what often appears in eco-poetry, indeed, what most ecopoets strive for, is a harmonization of place and space. Like Berry, Harjo, and Oliver, Merwin also seems to find this goal attractive. As he put it in a 1988 interview with David Elliot, a lack of place-awareness leads to a deprivation of reverence for the nonhuman world, which could potentially lead to the destruction of the earth:

> If we're so stupid that we choose to destroy each other and ourselves, that's bad enough; but if we destroy the whole life on the planet! And I'm not talking about a big bang; I'm talking about . . . the destruction of the seas, the destruction of species after species, the destruction of the forests. These are not replaceable. We can't suddenly decide years down the line that we made a mistake and put it all back. The feeling of awe —something that we seem to be losing—is essential for survival. ("IWSM" 6)

He made the same point in 1982 in an interview with Daniel Bourne. Responding to a question about his poetic and philosophical relationship to Robinson Jeffers, Merwin explained:

> The one thing I feel close to is his sense of our self-importance as a species, which I think is one of the things which is strangling us, our own bloated species-ego. The assumption that human beings are different in kind and in importance from other species is something I've had great difficulty accepting for twenty-five years or so. To me, it's a dangerously wrong way of seeing things. . . . If we make the distinction in a too self-flattering way, if we say we are the only kind of life that's of any importance, we automatically destroy our own importance. Our importance is based on a feeling of responsibility and awareness of all life. (Frazier 15)

What is necessary, in other words, is a space-conscious "awe" combined with and resulting from a place-centered commitment to the world itself.

Often Merwin is able to achieve such a synthesis in his verse. Consider, for example, the title poem from *The Vixen* (1996), in which the poet expresses his wonder at his encounter with a fox. The vixen becomes representative of the larger, nonhuman world Merwin loves, and the poem serves as something of a paean to the vixen, as the poet prays that his words "find their own / places" in the silence that follows his exposure to the animal world. We hear his enthusiastic fondness for the fox as he addresses her: "Even now you are unharmed even now perfect / as you have always been now when your light paws are running / on the breathless night on the bridge." Coupled with this sense of connection to the nonhuman world is Merwin's customary wonder at the ultimate unknowability of the vixen, whom he describes as an "aura of complete darkness," "keeper of the kept secrets / of the destroyed stories / the escaped dreams the sentences / never caught in words" (*Vixen* 69). In this lyric Merwin presents us with a model for a balanced combination of place and space: proceeding out of his passionate attachment to the vixen is an intense appreciation for the fox's dark, secretive, uncatchable nature.

This combination surfaces frequently in Merwin's verse. The first line of the first poem of *The River Sound*, which fittingly uses bridges as one of its primary symbols, establishes the place-space theme. In "Ceremony after an Amputation," the poet addresses "spirits of the place who were here before I saw it." With this line he asserts a point he repeatedly revisits in the collection: that his "place," the world around him, existed long before the individual speaker arrived to describe it or address it or even care for it.[3] This lone sentence articulates both Merwin's dedication to a Tuanian sense of place, as can be heard in the reverence with which he addresses the spirits of the place, and his recognition of the "spaciousness" of the larger world, in that it is greater than his ability to understand or communicate it. The space-consciousness remains present throughout the opening stanza; the speaker tells the spirits of place, "You have taught me without meaning," and he describes them as "unpronounceable as a face" (3).

"Waves in August" shows a similar intermingling of place and space. Merwin criticizes what he calls "that returning childish / wish to be living somewhere else," saying that he has evolved to a point where "now I find myself wishing / to be here to be alive here / it is impossible enough to still be the wish of a child." These lines demonstrate an attachment to place while also acknowledging the impossibility of maintaining the experience forever. This recognition has everything to do with lost innocence, as the rest of the poem makes clear. The speaker in the poem tells a story about hiding a boat near the water as a youth and coming back to discover that it had been stolen, leaving him not the boat, but "instead the sound of the water / with its whisper of vertigo // terror reassurance an old / old sadness." This sadness, the poem implies in its closing lines, is the stuff of adulthood and will remain with the speaker into his old age:

> it would seem we knew
> enough always about parting
> but we have to go on learning
> as long as there is anything (*RS* 125)

And the lesson that we go on learning, about sadness and parting and a lack of control over our world, materializes out of a desire to connect with that very world.

Take, as one final example of place-space synergy, a stanza from "Testimony" in which Merwin narrates (in third person) a moment from childhood when he looked from a hilltop over "a green valley that shone / with such light all the words were poor / later to tell what he had known" (*RS* 52). It is the wonder he feels regarding this experience with place that convinces him that the feeling is not articulable — "the words were poor." However, it is merely the articulation that is marred by linguistic limitation; the lack of sufficient words does not color or undermine the experience itself. Rather, the words are simply inadequate to render "what he had *known*." There is no uncertainty here. The space-consciousness is certainly present, but it co-exists with the poet's commitment to place.

Merwin, however, is often unable to present such a harmonizing vision in his poems, as his space-consciousness threatens to override his place sensibilities. Consider, for instance, the famous "For a Coming Extinction," in which Merwin addresses a gray whale that "we," humans, are sending to "the End." In this poem we see clearly the primary tension around which turns most of Merwin's ecopoetry. On one hand, the poet displays a postmodern awareness of language's inability to communicate something important. He tells the whale, "I write as though you could understand / And I could say it." Coupled with this is the absence of moral imperatives that results from a stripping away of transcendent foundations. The speaker ironically commands the whale that when it meets "that great god" at "the End," it must "tell him / That we who follow you invented forgiveness / And forgive nothing. . . . Tell him / That it is we who are important." Yet on the other hand, this postmodern skepticism regarding language and morality is problematized by an ecologically minded belief that there is something important that must be conveyed; that a real world, not just a mere poetic construction, is at stake. A real-life species is near extinction, and its eradication will "leav[e] behind it the future / Dead / And ours." The other casualties of this dead future include the "irreplaceable hosts ranged countless / And foreordaining as stars," creatures like "the sea cows the Great Auks the gorillas" (*SFB* 123).

Awareness of these often-conflicting issues places Merwin, along with other ecopoets, in a difficult situation. He is well aware of the linguistic and epistemological issues that have now come to bear on the current generation of poets and other thinkers, issues that call the very existence of "knowledge" and "truth" into question. Yet, simultaneously, he is also intensely aware of the importance of communicating *something*, and of the impending loss if he does not speak. These two sets of issues—both postmodern and ecological—form the crux of Merwin's difficulty in writing as a contemporary ecopoet. Jonathan Bate verbalizes this tension, asserting that "postmodernity proclaims that all marks are textmarks; ecopoetics proposes that we must hold fast to the possibility that certain textmarks called poems can bring back to our memory humankind's ancient knowledge that without landmarks we are lost" (175). And much of the evocative power of "For a Coming Extinction" and other Merwin poems stems from the fact that we hear both a place-consciousness and a space-consciousness, but with a striking dissonance between the two.

The problem for Merwin is not quite that his sense of place is overcome by his space-consciousness. In other words, it is not that he loses sight of his devotion to the nonhuman world and what occurs around him. Rather, his awareness of Tuanian space sometimes prevents him from fully articulating that devotion to place; thus, in his poems the harmony is not as apparent. We know from his other writings, and from many of his poems, that an attachment to place is crucial to his poetics. But his skepticism regarding human language, human intentions, and human knowledge is so great that he is doubtful of our ability to interact with, commit to, and communicate our place in the world as a home. We are like the people in "Frame" who see in a shop window a sign that reads "Today," "but what it was announcing was days ago," and "what it was there to say" has been forgotten, and "whatever is announced is over" (RS 123).

Most often, Merwin's skepticism centers on the familiar ecopoetic theme of language's inability to articulate accurately and fully the poet's experiences with the world. The words and their objects do not match up, for the words "never say / much of what they were meant to say" (RS 86). Frustration with this linguistic difficulty appears throughout the Merwin oeuvre. He speaks of "having a tongue / Of dust" and elsewhere calls the tongue "the black coat that fell off the wall / With sleeves trying to say something" (RS 83). He also depicts himself as an inept describer of the world: "My blind neighbor has required of me / A description of darkness / And I begin I begin . . ." ("The Gods," SFB 99). Cheri Davis offers what she calls "the basic existential, linguistic, and spiritual problem Merwin faces in his poetry":

> This is Merwin's parable for our time: After God created Adam and Eve, He instructed them to give names to the animals. He brought the animals to them one by one, and they were named. The names were magical in that they had rapport with the spiritual being of each animal, but unfortunately since then language has lost its original symbolic function. It, like man, fell. Call a wild animal by its name today. What happens? (42)

The problem is that the poet comprehends the communal nature of the world, and the connection that exists between himself and the animals, whom he regards as "the very embodiment of the miraculous in the common" (Davis 43); yet he feels that no language exists with which to assert the reality of this connection.

He conveys this frustration in the three-line poem "The Old Boast," from the aptly titled *Writings to an Unfinished Accompaniment*:

Listen natives of a dry place
from the harpist's fingers
rain (*SFB* 233)

In this complex lyric the poet indicates his awareness of his own limited powers. Although his poetry may approximate an individual version of reality, and in doing so musically slake the thirst of his audience, it is ultimately no more an accurate reproduction of reality than a harp's note is of actual rain. Thus we hear Merwin repeatedly bemoaning the fact that language (along with human understanding in general) is not up to the task of rendering an experience he has undergone. As he puts it, "The words I say / sometimes are heard another way / as nothing is dependable" (*RS* 87). Each experience is, in the words of the title of Merwin's fifth collection of poems, "the moving target."[4]

This issue is highlighted throughout Merwin's verse: even the form of his poems—the mazelike enjambment that turns virtually each line of each poem into something of a riddle; the almost complete lack of punctuation and capitalization; the often-cryptic titles; the difficult syntax—acknowledges the impossibility of "capturing" the poet's experience with the world around him. As Peter Davison puts it, Merwin abandons "the devices of journalism—the who-what-when-where-why" that traditionally provide context for the poem's subject. The form of the verse therefore "reinforce[s] the concept that experience surpasses the signifiers we ascribe to it, that the world itself is greater than the words with which we attempt to articulate our understanding of and connection to it." Put simply, the very *form* of the poems distances the reader from its content, thus further emphasizing disconnection.

IN RESPONSE TO this feeling of disconnection, Merwin's poems exhibit a fervent appreciation for silence, and the conclusion of many poems finds the speaker sitting in silence, listening, waiting, not speaking. For decades Merwin critics have discussed his use of silence, darkness, and absence in his poetry. As Richard Howard has said, "A silence lines his speech" (380). And Byers points out that this silence is "made literal in the poems' appearance on the page, with their short, halting lines, wide margins, frequent stanza breaks, and vast amounts of white space after the last word" (109). In Tuanian parlance, this silence proceeds out of a deep devotion to place and a resultant space-conscious humility in the face of the poet's inability to communicate or fully understand that place.

Take, for example, Merwin's narrative poem "Finding a Teacher," which opens with the speaker coming upon "an old friend fishing," of whom he asks a question. The friend answers only, "Wait." The speaker tells us that it was "a question about the sun / about my two eyes my ears my mouth / my heart the earth with its four seasons / my feet where I was standing / where I was going," and that "it slipped through my / hands as though it were water / into the river" and flowed away. The closing lines emphasize the lesson the speaker learned from the nonanswer he received from the fisherman:

I no longer knew what to ask
I could tell that his line had no hook
I understood that I was to stay and eat with him (*SFB* 285–286)

We see here the rational intellect being replaced by a respect for waiting and silence. The reason-based question appears, disappears, then dies away; then night falls, bringing with it the lesson of waiting and, symbolized by the unbaited hook, a voluntary surrender of control. Ultimately, the river becomes a *via negativa*, with even the lesson learned going unexpressed.

At times Merwin employs another form of silence, darkness. "By Day and by Night," from *The Moving Target,* suggests that the shadow, the "index of the sun," is in fact superior to its light, in that it is omnipresent, whereas the light is transitory. Addressing the shadow itself, Merwin writes that it sets up the sun's absence "like a camp. / And his fire only confirms you. And his death is your freedom" (*SFB* 14). In this preference for darkness over light Merwin affirms that it is often better to remain in shadow and silence than to make pronouncements concerning issues about which we cannot have more than limited knowledge.

In "Finally" the poet relates the moment he decides to confront his own darkness, which he calls "my dread, my ignorance, my / Self." He recognizes this unseen Self as his own identity, saying, "Come, no longer unthinkable. Let us share / Understanding like a family name." The speaker demonstrates his hope in the meaning that lies in this darkness: "Come. As a man who hears a sound at the gate / Opens the window and puts out the light / The better to see out into the dark, / Look, I put it out" (*SFB* 24). The speaker decides to confront and acknowledge his own "no longer unthinkable" and to accept that often the only authentic response to an experience with the world is to embrace and take refuge in the mystery of darkness and silence.

The alternative is to ignore the mystery, the shade, the absence, the silence. In "Native Trees," when the young poet asks his parents about the place they live and the names of the trees, they do not hear his questions, in fact do not even look where the boy points. Their attention is held so completely by their present, familiar surroundings that they no longer acknowledge the world's mystery: "across the room they could watch / walls they had forgotten / where there were no questions / no voices and no shade" (*RIT* 6). The absence of questions, voices, and shade means that frightening mystery is no longer acknowledged there, a mystery that of course appeals to the young Merwin but worries the parents who look to avoid such unknowns. The poem highlights the fact that a lack of a space-consciousness that embraces the unknown can lead to a lack of connection to place as well.

ULTIMATELY, THEN, as in most ecopoetry, place and space interact in Merwin's verse. The interaction leads to harmony at times, but more often the best the poet can do is to take refuge in silence. Still, the question for Merwin is how to honor his experience with the more-than-human world and still recognize his ultimate inability to communicate that experience. Scigaj writes that Merwin's poetry's "self-reflexiveness is very postmodern, but the thrust is not centripetal, toward the world of words as a self-contained synchronic system. It mourns the loss of a naïve encounter with nature as it foregrounds the impedence [*sic*] of language and conceptuality. It wishes it could recover something more from the silence, to convey the quality of a silent apprehension of the earth, and therefore the thrust is centrifugal, towards the nature that lies beyond the power of language" (183). This reading lines up well with the closing lines of "Testimony," where Merwin recounts the story of his mother showing him, as a boy, the Empire State Building. She instructs him to view the entire height of the building "as the time the earth existed / before life had begun on it," telling him that the lightning rod on the roof would then represent the short amount of time since life began. Switching metaphors, his mother compares the entire structure to a large book, explaining to the young Merwin that "the whole age when there had been / life of the kind we knew which we / came to call human and our own" would rest on top of "that closed book" "as thick as one stamp that might be / on a post card."

The poem closes with Merwin's characteristically questioning acceptance of mystery, as he and his mother walk along the street "over the stamp I had not seen":

> where would the card be going to
> that the stamp was to be put on
> would I see what was written down
> on it whenever it was sent
> and the few words what would they mean
> that we took with us as we went (*RS* 108)

The poem thus concludes with a question, and an unanswered one at that. Once again, mysterious silence reigns over Merwin's verse. Yet, as he said in the Folsom and Nelson interview, "the human can not exist independently in a natural void; whatever the alienation is that we feel from the natural world, we are not in fact alienated. . . . We're part of that whole thing" (323). The place-centered conviction that "we're part of that whole thing" pervades Merwin's writings. But because he can never move beyond his mother's space-conscious lesson of the postage stamp, his poetry tends toward silence.

CHAPTER SIX

The West Side of Any Mountain
Connections and Future Considerations

WE KNOW FROM HIS journals that during the latter part of 1841, a year that proved to be his most prolific period as a poet, Henry David Thoreau was considering abandoning poetry and adopting the natural essay as his primary mode of aesthetic expression. According to Elizabeth Hall Witherell, Thoreau, the literary ancestor of practically all ecopoets, "harbored fundamental doubts about both the vigor of poetry as opposed to prose and its suitability to his own temperament and particular talent" (59).[1] In February 1851, for example, he wrote, "The strains from my muse are as rare nowadays, or of late years, as the notes of birds in the winter, / —the faintest occasional tinkling sound, and mostly the woodpecker kind or the harsh jay or crow. It never melts into song" (Bode xi).

However, as Witherell makes clear, Thoreau's decision to forsake his poetic impulse resulted not only from his doubts concerning his own discordant muse, but also from his disenchantment with what were believed to be the greatest poems of his time, and with the ability of poetry in general to convey the true "Poetry" (in the Emersonian sense) of the natural world. These doubts sprang from his conviction that, while certain supreme artists like Homer had created poetry worthy of praise, most of what Thoreau called the "effeminate" lyrics of his contemporaries were vapid and impotent in their attempts to convey the wildness of the natural world. For instance, in late 1841, when Thoreau visited the Harvard College Library to select poems for an anthology he planned to edit, he experienced a deep disillusionment with respect to the work he discovered there in Cambridge. He wrote of "looking over the dry and dusty volumes of the English poets," and of his astonishment "that those fresh and fair creations I had imagined are contained in them. . . . I can hardly be serious with myself when I remember that I have come to Cam. after poetry—and while I am running over the catalogue, and collating and selecting—I think if it would not be a shorter way to a complete volume—to step at once into the field or wood, with a very low reverence to students and librarians" (30 November; *J1* 337–338).[2]

The undomesticated quality Thoreau searched for was largely absent from both his own work and that of his most talented contemporaries. As he wrote in a journal entry from early 1851, "The best poets, after all, exhibit only a tame and civil side of nature—They have not seen the west side of any mountain. Day and night—mountain and wood are visible from the wilderness as well as the village—They have their primeval aspects—sterner savager—than any poet has sung. It is only the white man's poetry—we want the Indian's report. Wordsworth is too tame for the Chippeway" (18 August; *J1* 321). This frustration with the inability of "the white man's poetry" to celebrate the "sterner savager" characteristics of nonhuman nature served as a major contributor to Thoreau's ultimate abandonment of poetry.

Readers familiar with Thoreau will notice the similarities between the characteristics of ecopoetry—ecocentrism, an appreciation of wildness, and a skepticism toward hyperrationality and its resultant overreliance on technology—and the principles that dominate *Walden* and the majority of the Thoreau canon. Just as Thoreau voiced his displeasure with "white man's poetry" and offered his prose writings in response, much of contemporary nature poetry has been transformed into more ecologically aware verse that attempts to address existing environmental issues and to portray faithfully the "place-ness" as well as the wildness of the natural world.

My goal in these readings of ecopoets and their work has been to further define the field and to map some of its key tendencies and characteristics, demonstrating in it a certain continuity. In each writer's poetry we perceive an intense desire to respond to the modern crisis associated with Cartesian dualism. The project of each is to recover a sense of the world as one organism made up of symbiotic components, both human and nonhuman. In all four poets this vision is manifest in a sympathy for the nonhuman other that leads to a recognition of a kinship between humans and the rest of the natural world, and to an awareness of the human inability ever to understand or articulate the other.

Within these parallels striking differences appear. For instance, the subject matter each poet typically chooses differs greatly. Berry's characteristic poem "Where," narrating the ruination of Lane's Landing, is much different from Oliver's "Landscape," about spiritually patient sheets of moss; and both of these contrast sharply with Harjo's "Deer Dancer," with its urban "bar of broken survivors," and with Merwin's "Airport," about the aspatial building that "is not a place / but a container with signs / directing a process."

Significant differences also appear when we examine the poets' strategies for (at least partially) overcoming modern dualism. Berry, Harjo, Oliver, and Merwin all look to reunite human and nonhuman worlds; in short, they are all place-makers attempting to portray the world as place and home. Yet their approaches to this goal are notably different, as is the extent to which they demonstrate self-consciousness regarding that objective. Oliver appears to be more aware than Berry or Harjo of the difficulties involved in "going back," in returning to a non- or less-dualistic existence. All four poets display this recognition; indeed, the very idea of Tuanian space, prevalent in each poet's work, presupposes an understanding of our ultimate inability to comprehend fully or reunite with the nonhuman world. However, while both Berry and Harjo emphasize their own space-consciousness, neither foregrounds this insight to the extent that Oliver does, as in her self-conscious use of the pathetic fallacy. And Merwin goes beyond even Oliver in his awareness of space, ultimately consigning his poetry to the realm of silence itself.

Place and space often determine formal issues in the poetry as well. Berry, for instance, is an extremely controlled poet, utilizing traditional forms and measured lines, creating a recognizable and comfortable place within his work. Harjo's verse, on the other hand, often plays the trickster role in refusing to obey conventional patterns, sometimes (more and more, lately) even refusing to adhere to generic conventions regarding categories like prose and poetry. The lines in Oliver's ecopoems sometimes flow like the sea they describe, and often, as John Elder points out, her poetry eschews anything like final closure by offering "short, pulsing lines" that "allow for a non-hierarchical clustering of images" (221). And Merwin's largely nonexistent punctuation and unconventional capitalization emphasize the breaking down of language, resulting finally in silence, embodied in the large areas of white space surrounding the letters on the page. His verse often gives the impression, in the words of David Gilcrest, that it has "accept[ed] the self-exile of language" (149).

All signs point to the continued proliferation of ecopoetry, for poetry has always been a sign of the times, a representation of current issues and problems; and the times in which we now live require, even demand, that we pay attention to our relationship with the natural world and attempt to deal with the human/nature divorce we have created. It seems significant that 150 years after Thoreau began to give up on poetry, we are only now, within the last few decades, producing a significant body of poetic work that takes into account many of the issues that so concerned him. The cause for this delay is uncertain. Perhaps he was right to doubt "the vigor of poetry as opposed to prose"; or perhaps poetry's evolution, like our society's mindset, is slow to catch up to this aspect of his vision. But whatever the reason, more and more poets are now attempting to produce work that draws near to what Thoreau called "the west side of any mountain." Whether or not he would say that these poets have seen that west side is open to question; but it seems likely that he would have a greater chance of discovering a "westward-looking" poetry in today's libraries than he had in 1841. For contemporary ecopoets are at least making the effort to create poems that make place by portraying the transhuman world as home while also remaining mindful of space in nature's "sterner savager" aspects. They are now making the effort to view the mountain "from the wilderness as well as the village."

Notes

Preface

1. Critical discussions of the convergence of poetry and ecology have indeed appeared for years, primarily in the work of scholars like Patrick Murphy, Sherman Paul, and Len Scigaj. However, excepting a few such studies, ecocritical or environmentally minded criticism has largely ignored poetry. For years only two book-length studies of the field of contemporary nature poetry were available: John Elder's compelling and widely read *Imagining the Earth: Poetry and the Vision of Nature* and Terry Gifford's important *Green Voices: Understanding Contemporary Nature Poetry*.

Two other studies of note appeared in 1991, Guy Rotella's *Reading and Writing Nature: The Poetry of Robert Frost, Wallace Stevens, Marianne Moore, and Elizabeth Bishop*, and Jonathan Bate's *Romantic Ecology: Wordsworth and the Environmental Tradition*. Each provides a good introduction to some of the issues facing contemporary poets of nature, although neither actually focuses on working ecopoets. Several nature-poetry anthologies have also become available in the last few years, but these are for the most part collections of poems rather than treatments of the mode. See, for instance, Robert Bly's *News of the Universe: Poems of a Twofold Consciousness*; Sara Dunn and Alan Scholefield's *Beneath the Wide Wide Heaven: Poetry of the Environment from Antiquity to the Present*; Christopher Merrill's *The Forgotten Language: Contemporary Poets and Nature*; Robert Pack and Jay Parini's *Poems for a Small Planet: Contemporary American Nature Poetry*; and John Daniel's *Wild Song: Poems of the Natural World*.

Over the last few years several books have examined contemporary nature poetry generally and ecopoetry specifically, among them Gyorgyi Voros's *Notations of the Wild: Ecology in the Poetry of Wallace Stevens* (1997); Len Scigaj's *Sustainable Poetry: Four Ecopoets* (1999); Bate's *Song of the Earth* (2000); Bernie Quetchenbach's *Back from the Far Field: American Nature Poets in the Late Twentieth Century* (2000); David Gilcrest's *Greening the Lyre: Environmental Poetics and Ethics* (2002); and Jed Rasula's *This Compost: Ecological Imperatives in American Poetry* (2002). Murphy's edited *Literature of Nature: An International Sourcebook* (1998) offers ecocritical treatment of several examples of world nature poetry. In addition, my edited volume *Ecopoetry: A Critical Introduction* (2002) gathers some of the most significant (as well as emerging) critical voices working in the field.

Three recent dissertations may also be noted: George Hart's "The Poetics of Postmodernist and Neoromantic Nature Poetry" (Stanford University, 1997); Laird Christiansen's "Spirit Astir in the World: Sacred Poetry in the Age of Ecology" (University of Oregon, 1999); and my own "Place and Space in Contemporary Ecological Poetry: Berry, Harjo, and Oliver" (University of Kentucky, 1999), out of which the present volume has grown. One other valuable venue offering work on ecopoetics has been the journal *ISLE: Interdisciplinary Studies of Literature and the Environment*.

2. As Scigaj puts it, "If environmental writers constitute a smaller group within the class of nature writers, ecopoets comprise an even smaller subgroup within the environmentalist group" (11). Ecopoets and environmental poets are alike, however, in that in their work "language is often foregrounded only to reveal its limitations, and this is accomplished in such a way that the reader's gaze is thrust beyond language back into the less limited natural world that language refers to, the inhabited place where humans must live in harmony with ecological cycles" (38).

1. All Finite Things Reveal Infinitude

1. For excellent descriptions of the myriad studies of place in a wide variety of disciplines, see the introductions to Franklin and Steiner's *Mapping American Culture* (1992) and Feld and Basso's *Senses of Place* (1996).

2. The artist Alan Gussow supports this definition in his discussion of the relation between "place" and "environment":

> In thinking about the conservation of *environment*, I gradually came to realize that an environment was not a place; that the words were not interchangeable; and that the difference was critical. There is a great deal of talk these days about saving the environment. We must, for the environment sustains our bodies. But as humans we also require support for our spirits, and this is what certain kinds of places provide. . . . Viewed simply as a life-support system, the earth is an environment. Viewed as a resource that sustains our humanity, the earth is a collection of places. (27)

And these places, as the sociologist Harvey Molotch puts it, are made up of all the stuff of life, for "interpenetrations of daily rounds and high culture, ways of life and circulating beliefs, are raw materials of what can come from place" (225).

3. Certain ecopoets, biologists, Gaia hypothesis proponents, and adherents to

new age philosophy and religion represent the closest modern Westerners come to asserting an organic view of the world.

4. Of course, love of a place does not guarantee that we will not harm it. As Wallace Stegner once wrote in his essay "Thoughts in a Dry Land," "I really only want to say that we may love a place and still be dangerous to it." He makes this statement just after asking whether "Lewis and Clark shouldn't have been made to file an environmental impact study before they started west."

5. In an article entitled "Is Humanity Suicidal?" Wilson defines "exemptionalism" as the belief that "since humankind is transcendent in intelligence and spirit, so must our species have been released from the iron laws of ecology that bind all other species. No matter how serious the problem, civilized human beings, by ingenuity, force of will and—who knows?—divine dispensation, will find a solution" (27).

6. As Berry puts it, "Form, [Ammons] believes, is in all things, but the forms comprehended in nature or achieved in art are necessarily partial forms, fragments, inferior to the form of the whole creation, which can be neither comprehended nor imagined" (CH 33). This aspect of Ammons's work echoes Snyder's reminder that we are "hemmed in by mysteries / all moving in order" ("The Manicheans," BC 76).

2. Divided against Ourselves

1. Many of Berry's marriage poems are traditional love poems that refer to his actual marriage to Tanya Berry. Since these poems are relevant only peripherally here, I concentrate primarily on those poems in which marriage applies to place-making.

2. The standard text concerning wilderness and its relationship to civilization is Roderick Nash's *Wilderness and the American Mind*. Other good introductions to this problematic can be found in Hans Peter Duerr's *Dreamtime: Concerning the Boundary between Wilderness and Civilization*; Peter J. Wilson's *The Domestication of the Human Species*; William Cronon's *Uncommon Ground: Rethinking the Human Place in Nature*; and Oelschlaeger's *The Wilderness Condition: Essays on Environment and Civilization*.

3. Oelschlaeger states that "experience of the wilderness as an 'other' is necessary to any grounded understanding of human beingness and articulation of individual identity" (8–9). For fuller discussions of this argument, see Duerr's *Dreamtime*, Paul Shepard's *Thinking Animals: Animals and the Development of Human Intelligence*, and Konrad Lorenz's *Studies in Animal and Human Behavior*.

4. Alison Byerly discusses this linguistic dilemma in her analysis of the National Park system, asserting that "the idea of wilderness refers to the absence of humanity, yet 'wilderness' has no meaning outside the context of the civilization that defines it. This paradox requires that we experience the wilderness without changing its status *as* wilderness. This can only be done by constructing an aesthetic image of the

wilderness that allows us to avoid confronting its reality" (54). Byerly exposes the inherent contradiction within the 1964 Wilderness Act itself, which established national parks that were to be "administered for the use and enjoyment of the American people," but only "in such a manner as will leave them unimpaired for future use and enjoyment as wilderness" (Allin 277). Byerly points out that "the Wilderness Act's own definition of wilderness reveals the paradox involved. The visitor to a wilderness area should find a place that has not been visited" (57).

5. Berry elsewhere reiterates Silko's point, arguing that "the idea that we live in something called 'the environment' . . . is utterly preposterous," for "'environment' means that which surrounds or encircles us; it means a world separate from ourselves, outside of." He maintains that "the real state of things, of course, is far more complex and intimate and interesting than that. The world that environs us, that is around us, is also within us. We are made of it; we eat, drink, and breathe it; it is bone of our bone and flesh of our flesh." In fact, Berry claims, the very word "environment" "is a typical product of the old dualism that is at the root of most of our ecological destructiveness" (*SEFC* 34).

6. The traditional concept of the great chain of being, with its placement of humanity above the rest of nature in a cosmological hierarchy, is not usually a popular one in environmental circles. Berry looks to revive appreciation for the chain by phrasing it in a way more palatable to contemporary environmentalists. He writes, "What the old believers in the Chain of Being have to say to us is that if we conceive ourselves as the subjects of God, whose law is in part the law of nature, then there is some hope that we can right ourselves and behave with decency within the community of creatures. We will be spared the clumsiness, waste, and grave danger of trying to make up our own rules" (*SBW* 136). The medievalist Christopher Manes confirms this characterization, writing that "for the medieval exegete, the Great Chain of Being at times acted as a theological restraint against abusing the natural world, at least within the hushed, abstracted cells of the cloister" (20). He quotes Thomas Aquinas:

> The goodness of the species transcends the goodness of the individual, as form transcends matter; therefore the multiplication of species is a greater addition to the good of the universe than the multiplication of individuals of a single species. The perfection of the universe therefore requires not only a multitude of individuals, but also diverse kinds, and therefore diverse grades of things. (20)

Berry recognizes the accusations of arrogance he invites by proposing that we view ourselves as caretakers of the natural world and responds:

> Implicit in the Chain of Being is the idea that creatures are protected in their various kinds, not by equality, but by difference; and that if humans are respon-

sibly observant of the differences between themselves and the angels above them and the animals below, they will act with respect, restraint, and benevolence toward the subordinate creatures; this is their duty toward the subordinate creatures, and it is part of, inseparable from, their duty to the higher creatures and to God. (*SBW* 168).

Berry's point mirrors Turner's assertion that "that ecological modesty which asserts that we are only one species among many, with no special rights, we may now see as the abdication of a trust. We are, whether we like it or not, the lords of creation; true humility consists not in pretending that we aren't, but in living up to the trust that it implies by service to the greater glory and beauty of the world we have been given to look after. It is a bad shepherd who, on democratic principles, deserts his sheep" ("Cultivating" 50). "The question is not," writes Berry, "one of ecological egalitarianism or pacifism, but of harmony between part and whole" (*SBW* 141). And this "ecological" chain of being, Berry believes, offers the best chance for such harmony.

7. Incidentally, these values preside over Berry's fiction as well. As Quetchenbach points out, Berry's character Burley Coulter is described as "a man of two loves, not always compatible: of the dark woods, and of the daylit membership of kin and friends and households" (Berry *WB* 127).

8. For example, the human body, argues Berry, is "half wild, for it is dependent upon reflexes, instincts, and appetites that we do not cause or intend and that we cannot, or had better not, stop." He asserts that

we live, partly, because we are domestic creatures—that is, we participate in our human economy to the extent that we "make a living"; we are able, with variable success, to discipline our appetites and instincts in order to produce this artifact, this human living. And yet it is equally true that we breathe and our hearts beat and we survive as a species because we are wild. (*HE* 139–140)

3. Finding the Way Back

1. This applies especially to the English language, as Paula Gunn Allen points out:

In English, one can divide the universe into two parts: the natural and the supernatural. Humanity has no real part in either, being neither animal nor spirit—that is, the supernatural is discussed as though it were apart from people, and the natural as though people were apart from it. This necessarily forces English-speaking people into a position of alienation from the world they live in. Such isolation is entirely foreign to American Indian thought. At base, every story, every song, every ceremony tells the Indian that each creature is part of a living whole and that all parts of that whole are related to one another by virtue of their participation in the whole of being. (60)

For another, more detailed expression of this argument, see chapter 3 of David Abram's *The Spell of the Sensuous*; he argues that "in indigenous, oral cultures, . . . language seems to encourage and augment the participatory life of the senses, while in Western civilization language seems to deny or deaden that life, promoting a massive distrust of sensorial experience while valorizing an abstract realm of ideas hidden behind or beyond the sensory appearances" (71–72).

2. Harjo's use of the term "mythic" corresponds to Allen's definition of the word. As Allen notes in *The Sacred Hoop*, "mythic" can refer to "narratives that deal with metaphysical, spiritual, and cosmic occurrences that recount the spiritual past and the 'mysteries' of the tribe"; or to the "sacred story. The *Word* in its cosmic, creative sense. This usage follows the literary meaning rather than the common or vernacular meaning of 'fictive' or 'not real narrative dealing with primitive, irrational explanations of the world'" (274).

3. This seems a good place to acknowledge the problematic nature of my writing about Harjo's tribal heritage and her attempts to recover it. As an Anglo myself and therefore necessarily an outsider, I must receive Harjo's Native vision of the world second- or even third-hand. However, it is also clear that for Harjo, a mixed-blood writer herself, this process of (and need for) going back is not restricted to Native Americans. She makes it abundantly clear that Europeans were once tribal peoples and have also lost a great deal ("Weaving" 128).

4. As an example of a Harjo poem that takes the spiral as its climactic image, consider the following untitled prose poem, from *Secrets from the Center of the World*:

Near Shiprock five horses stand at the left side of the road, watching traffic. A pole carrying talk cuts through the middle of the world. They notice the smoking destruction from the Four Corners plant as it veers overhead, shake their heads at the ways of the thoughtless humans, lope toward the vortex of circling sands where a pattern for survival is fiercely stated. (16)

5. For additional discussion of "Grace," see Murphy (*LNO* 86–87) and Nancy Lang ("Through Landscape" 158).

6. For a discussion of feminist tricksters in Harjo, see Holmes.

7. Harjo has said that we have many more than five senses:

In European culture the world is supposed to have only three dimensions. It's constructed in a way that only the five senses can maneuver. There are probably more than five senses; there are probably ten, twelve, fourteen, a hundred senses—and we haven't developed them. ("Laughter" 136)

Lang has suggested an alternative explanation for Harjo's surrealism, arguing that it is a response to her recognition of the reality that "while *who* holds power over others may change, oppression remains" (47–48). Sometimes this "clownish humor"

> may temporarily relieve this surreal tension, but such humor is not the Eurocentric, Bakhtinian-related carnivalization of explosive laughter leading to release and relaxation. Rather, Native American clownish humor may often deliberately play the Fool in order to mask and subvert rising hysteria. For example, in "The Book of Myths," . . . both the speaker and Rabbit struggle to stay alive and hang on to their self-control in a dangerous place; and foolish behavior and stories help to keep terror at bay. (48)

4. Both Sides of the Beautiful Water

1. Notice that Abram does not claim that the nonhuman world seems more beautiful and alive because it *cares* for him, only that his own body's reaction to that world determines the way he sees it and interacts with it. This is important in considering Oliver's use of the pathetic fallacy.

2. Since phenomenology itself is not my primary concern in this chapter, I am offering a largely elliptical explanation, setting down only the most basic points that will aid in exploring the work of Oliver.

3. This tendency of Oliver to link herself with nature has caused a good deal of discussion among feminist scholars, indeed, more discussion by far than any other element of her work. The debate centers around the contentious question of an inherent link between women and nature. For good introductions to the issues, see Bonds and McNew.

4. As I noted in chapter 3, Berry recommends maintaining a perspective founded on an "updated, ecological version of the chain of being" that situates people in a relationship with the rest of nature and stresses our responsibility based on that relationship. Recall that he argues that "what the old believers in the Chain of Being have to say to us is that if we conceive ourselves as the subjects of God, whose law is in part the law of nature, then there is some hope that we can right ourselves and behave with decency within the community of creatures. We will be spared the clumsiness, waste, and grave danger of trying to make up our own rules" (*SBW* 136). I'm not sure that Berry and Abram (and Harjo, for that matter) are really too far apart in their positions here, but Berry's response to the criticism offered by Abram and Harjo seems to me a persuasive one.

5. Robin Riley Fast discusses this celebrated indistinguishability in Oliver, noting that the relationship between Oliver's speakers and the natural world is analogous to what, in human relationships, Evelyn Fox Keller calls "dynamic autonomy." Fast quotes Keller's explanation that "dynamic autonomy is a product at least as much of relatedness as it is of delineation"; as such, it "enables the very real indeterminacy in the distinction between subject and object to function as a resource rather than as a source of confusion and threat" (Keller 99). Dynamic autonomy, writes Keller, "presupposes that the fears of merging, the loss of boundaries, on the one hand, and the fears of loneliness and disconnection, on the other, can be balanced. It also presupposes the compatibility of one's contrasting desires for intimacy and independence" (100).

6. Notice the implicit erotics within this poem, with its references to the tactility of the other's skin, to the "legs which tremble / and open / into the dark country / I keep dreaming of," to the intimate journey across the body. The sexualized merging we observe here (and elsewhere in Oliver's work, for instance in "Blossom" and "Music") depicts poet and nature as intimate lovers in a passionate relationship. Oliver's portrayal is much different from earlier nature poets who write about ravishing nature or being ravished by it. Recall, for instance, Wordsworth's rape of the silent bower in "Nutting," or Guyon's destruction of the Bower of Bliss in Spenser's *Faerie Queene*. Whereas these earlier authors often emphasized violence and dominance in the power relationship between human and nature, Oliver assumes as her starting point an intersubjective world based on an intimate and respectful relationship between fellow subjects.

7. I should point out that Graham insists that for Oliver, "this loss of self is never permanent":

> Oliver becomes, in turns, a bear, a whale, a fish, but, as each poem and each subsequent transformation suggests, she returns again to human consciousness and must repeat the process of becoming another over and over. . . . She cannot resign herself to being just "the dog in the dog" because this would mean she could never be a bear or a fish. Giving up human subjectivity would mean, at least as Oliver perceives it, giving up the ability to mime herself into the body of another. It would also mean giving up self-consciousness, knowing who and what she is, as well as the ability to remember and write about the experience. (366)

Similarly, Fast argues that what Oliver "yearns for is visionary knowledge, attained through a dissolution of boundaries between self and other, self and nature, that enables a larger, more dynamic, more empowering knowledge of self and other, in relationship" (Fast 376).

8. More evidence that Oliver is employing the fallacy intentionally is that she has increasingly turned to the device as her career and work have matured. The 1972

The River Styx, Ohio, and Other Poems, for instance, contains only the occasional personification, as in "Mr. Frost's Chickens." Oliver's 1997 *West Wind*, in contrast, has personification on virtually every page. My point here is not, of course, that personification is evidence of Oliver's maturing poetic ability, but rather that her choice to give voice to her nonhuman natural subjects has been a conscious and evolving one. As she explains in her *Poetry Handbook*, the only real problem with personification occurs when it is misused, or poorly used:

> Personification is an enlivening and joyful device. The challenge, of course, is to do it well. What you say about the abstraction or inanimate object must make sense of some sort. . . . Simply to have trees wave, or waves dance, will not do. Better no personification than bad or foolish personification. (104)

Oliver herself has, incidentally, been accused of "bad" personification. Fast writes that in Oliver's "Sunday Morning, High Tide" (*TM* 54), "the pathetic fallacy belies the acknowledgment of otherness, of alien if wondrous power" and thus robs the sea of its force.

9. In the title poem of *West Wind* (1997), Oliver describes herself as a translator or interpreter of nature, addressing herself as one "puddled in lamplight at your midnight desk — / you there, rewriting nature / so anyone can understand it" (49).

10. *Webster's Ninth New Collegiate Dictionary*.

5. Between the Earth and Silence

1. Sandra M. Guy provides a reading of this poem, along with an examination of Merwin's use of the four elements.

2. See also "Harm's Way," "Wanting to See," and "Testimony."

3. See, for instance, "Harm's Way," "Wanting to See," and "Chorus" for other poems that highlight this theme.

4. Scigaj makes a similar point in his discussion of Heidegger, noting that "even the most successful poetic quest leaves the quester cognizant of the fact that language does not reveal its origins, and Being conceals as it reveals glimpses" (181).

6. The West Side of Any Mountain

1. My reading of Thoreau's poetry is heavily indebted to Witherell's scholarship.

2. References to Thoreau's journal are from *Journal One: 1837–1844* (Princeton: Princeton University Press, 1981), ed. Elizabeth Hall Witherell et al., cited in this chapter as *J1*.

Bibliography

Abram, David. *The Spell of the Sensuous: Perception and Language in a More-Than-Human World*. New York: Vintage, 1997.

Allen, Paula Gunn. *The Sacred Hoop: Recovering the Feminine in American Indian Traditions*. Boston: Beacon, 1992.

Allin, Craig W. *The Politics of Wilderness Preservation*. Westport, CT: Greenwood, 1982.

Ammons, A. R. *The Selected Poems*. Expanded ed. New York: Norton, 1986.

Angyal, Andrew J. *Wendell Berry*. New York: Twayne, 1995.

Baker, David. Review of *House of Light*, by Mary Oliver. *Kenyon Review* 13.1 (Winter 1991): 192–202.

Barber, David. Review of *Entries*, by Wendell Berry. *Poetry* 166.1 (April 1995): 38–42.

Barge, Laura. "Changing Forms of the Pastoral in Southern Poetry." *Southern Literary Journal* 26.1 (Fall 1993): 30-41.

Barnhart, Robert K. *The Barnhart Dictionary of Etymology*. New York: Wilson, 1988.

Basney, Lionel. "Having Your Meaning at Hand: Work in Snyder and Berry." *Word, Self, Poem: Essays on Contemporary Poetry from the "Jubilation of Poets."* Ed. Leonard M. Trawick. Kent, OH: Kent State UP, 1990. 130–143.

Basso, Keith. *Wisdom Sits in Places: Landscape and Language among the Western Apache*. Albuquerque: U of New Mexico P, 1996.

———. "Wisdom Sits in Places: Landscape and Language among the Western Apache." *Senses of Place*. Ed. Steven Feld and Keith H. Basso. Santa Fe: School of American Research Press, 1996.

Bate, Jonathan. "Poetry and Biodiversity." *Writing the Environment: Ecocriticism and Literature*. Ed. Richard Kerridge and Neil Sammells. London: Zed Books, 1998.

———. *Romantic Ecology: Wordsworth and the Environmental Tradition*. New York: Routledge, 1991.

―――. *Song of the Earth*. Cambridge: Harvard UP, 2000.

Beach, Joseph Warren. *The Concept of Nature in Nineteenth-Century English Poetry*. New York: Macmillan, 1956.

Berman, Morris. *The Reenchantment of the World*. Toronto: Bantam, 1984.

Berry, Wendell. *Another Turn of the Crank*. Washington, D.C.: Counterpoint, 1995.

―――. *Clearing*. New York: Harcourt Brace, 1977.

―――. *Collected Poems: 1957–1982*. New York: North Point, 1984.

―――. *A Continuous Harmony*. New York: Harcourt Brace, 1972.

―――. *The Country of Marriage*. San Diego: Harvest, 1973.

―――. *Entries*. New York: Pantheon, 1994.

―――. *Farming: A Handbook*. San Diego: Harvest, 1970.

―――. *Home Economics*. San Francisco: North Point, 1987.

―――. *Long-Legged House*. New York: Harcourt Brace, 1969.

―――. "The Obligation of Care." *Sierra* 80 (September–October 1995): 62–67.

―――. *A Part*. San Francisco: North Point, 1980.

―――. *Recollected Essays*. San Francisco: North Point, 1981.

―――. *Sabbaths*. San Francisco: North Point, 1987.

―――. *Sex, Economy, Freedom, and Community*. New York: Pantheon, 1992.

―――. *Standing by Words*. San Francisco: North Point, 1983.

―――. *A Timbered Choir: The Sabbath Poems, 1979–1997*. Washington, DC: Counterpoint, 1999.

―――. *The Unsettling of America*. New York: Avon, 1977.

―――. *The Wild Birds: Six Stories of the Port William Membership*. San Francisco: North Point, 1989.

Bloom, Harold. "The New Transcendentalism: The Visionary Strain in Merwin, Ashbery, and Ammons." *Chicago Review* 24. 3 (Winter 1973): 25–43.

Bly, Robert, ed. *News of the Universe: Poems of Twofold Consciousness*. San Francisco: Sierra Club Books, 1980.

―――. *What Have I Ever Lost by Dying?* New York: HarperCollins, 1992.

Bode, Carl. Introduction. *Collected Poems of Henry Thoreau*. Ed. Carl Bode. Baltimore: Johns Hopkins UP, 1964.

Bonds, Diane S. "The Language of Nature in the Poetry of Mary Oliver." *Women's Studies* 21 (1992): 1–15.

Brunner, Edward J. *Poetry as Labor and Privilege: The Writings of W. S. Merwin*. Urbana: U of Illinois P, 1991.

Bryson, J. Scott, ed. *Ecopoetry: A Critical Introduction*. Salt Lake City: University of Utah P, 2002.

―――. "Place and Space in Contemporary Ecological Poetry: Berry, Harjo, and Oliver." PhD diss., University of Kentucky, 1999.

Buber, Martin. *I and Thou:* New York: Touchstone, 1970.

Buell, Lawrence. *The Environmental Imagination: Thoreau, Nature Writing, and the Formation of American Culture.* Cambridge: Harvard UP, 1995.

Burton-Christie, Douglas. "Nature, Spirit, and Imagination in the Poetry of Mary Oliver." *Cross Currents* 46.1 (1996): 77–87.

Byerly, Allison. "The Uses of Landscape: The Picturesque Aesthetic and the National Park System." *The Ecocriticism Reader: Landmarks in Literary Ecology.* Ed. Cheryll Glotfelty and Harold Fromm. Athens: U of Georgia P, 1996. 52–68.

Byers, Thomas B. *What I Cannot Say: Self, Word, and World in Whitman, Stevens, and Merwin.* Urbana: U of Illinois P, 1989.

Capra, Fritjof. *The Tao of Physics: An Exploration of the Parallels between Modern Physics and Eastern Mysticism.* 1975. 3rd ed. Boston: Shambhala, 1991.

———. *The Turning Point: Science, Society, and the Rising Culture.* New York: Bantam, 1983.

Casey, Edward S. *The Fate of Place: A Philosophic History.* Berkeley: U of California P, 1996.

———. *Getting Back into Place: Toward a Renewed Understanding of the Place-World.* Bloomington: Indiana UP, 1993.

———. "How to Get from Space to Place in a Fairly Short Stretch of Time: Phenomenological Prolegomena." *Senses of Place.* Ed. Steven Feld and Keith H. Basso. Santa Fe: School of American Research P, 1996. 13–52.

Christiansen, Laird. "Spirit Astir in the World: Sacred Poetry in the Age of Ecology." PhD diss., University of Oregon, 1999.

Christhilf, Mark. *W. S. Merwin the Mythmaker.* Columbia: U of Missouri P, 1986.

Cokinos, Christopher. "The Gaian Muse: Nature Poetry at the End of Nature." *Kansas Quarterly* 24–25 (1992–1993): 171–194.

Collingwood, R. G. *The Idea of Nature.* London: Oxford UP, 1960.

Collins, Robert. "A More Mingled Music: Wendell Berry's Ambivalent View of Language." *Modern Poetry Studies* 11 (1982): 35–56.

Coltelli, Laura. "Introduction: The Transforming Power of Joy Harjo's Poetry." *The Spiral of Memory.* Ed. Laura Coltelli. Ann Arbor: U of Michigan P, 1996. 1–13.

Costello, Bonnie. "On Poetry and the Idea of Nature." *Dædalus: Journal of the American Academy of Arts and Sciences* 132.1 (Winter 2003): 131–135.

———. *Shifting Ground: Reinventing Landscape in Modern American Poetry.* Cambridge: Harvard UP, 2003.

Crawford, John F. "Notes toward a New Multicultural Criticism: Three Works by Women of Color." *A Gift of Tongues: Critical Challenges in Contemporary American Poetry.* Ed. Marie Harris and Kathleen Aguero. Athens: U of Georgia P, 1987. 155–195.

Cronon, William. *Uncommon Ground : Rethinking the Human Place in Nature.* New York: Norton, 1996.

Daniel, John, ed. *Wild Song: Poems of the Natural World.* Athens: U of Georgia P, 1998.

Davis, Cheri. *W. S. Merwin.* Boston: Twayne, 1981.

Davison, Peter. "Merwin Hears the Immortality of Echo." Review of *The River Sound*, by W. S. Merwin. *Boston Globe*, 24 January 1999, sec. G, p. 3.

Dawkins, Richard. *Unweaving the Rainbow: Science, Delusion, and the Appetite for Wonder.* Boston: Houghton Mifflin, 1998.

Deloria, Philip J. *Playing Indian.* New Haven: Yale UP, 1998.

Devall, Bill, and George Sessions, eds. *Deep Ecology: Living As If Nature Mattered.* Salt Lake City: Peregrine Smith, 1985.

Dillard, Annie. *Pilgrim at Tinker Creek.* Toronto: Bantam, 1974.

Donovan, Kathleen McNerney. "Dark Continent / Dark Woman: Transformation and Healing in the Work of Hélène Cixous and Joy Harjo." *Native American Literatures.* Ed. Laura Coltelli. Pisa, Italy: SEU, 1994. 51–63.

Dresser, Nathaniel. "Cultivating Wilderness: The Place of Land in the Fiction of Ed Abbey and Wendell Berry." *Growth and Change* 26 (Summer 1995): 350–364.

Duerr, Hans Peter. *Dreamtime: Concerning the Boundary between Wilderness and Civilization.* Trans. Felicitas Goodman. New York: Basil Blackwell, 1987.

Dunn, Sara, and Alan Scholefield, eds. *Beneath the Wide Wide Heaven: Poetry of the Environment from Antiquity to the Present.* London: Virago, 1991.

Easlea, Brian. *Witch Hunting, Magic, and the New Philosophy: An Introduction to Debates of the Scientific Revolution.* Brighton, Sussex: Harvester P, 1980.

Ehrenfeld, David. *The Arrogance of Humanism.* New York: Oxford UP, 1978.

Einstein, Albert. *The World as I See It.* New York: Citadel Press, 1993.

Elder, John. *Imagining the Earth: Poetry and the Vision of Nature.* Urbana: U of Illinois P, 1985.

Emerson, Ralph Waldo. *The Collected Works of Ralph Waldo Emerson.* Ed. Alfred R. Ferguson and Robert E. Spiller. Cambridge: Harvard UP, 1971.

Evernden, Neil. "Beyond Ecology: Self, Place, and the Pathetic Fallacy." *The Ecocriticism Reader: Landmarks in Literary Ecology.* Ed. Cheryll Glotfelty and Harold Fromm. Athens: U of Georgia P, 1996. 92–104.

———. *The Social Creation of Nature.* Baltimore: Johns Hopkins UP, 1992.

Fast, Robin Riley. "Moore, Bishop, and Oliver: Thinking Back, Re-Seeking the Sea." *Twentieth Century Literature* 39.3 (Fall 1993): 364–379.

Feld, Steven, and Keith H. Basso, eds. *Senses of Place.* Santa Fe: School of American Research P, 1996.

Fitter, Chris. *Poetry, Space, Landscape: Toward a New Theory.* New York: Cambridge UP, 1995.

Foerster, Norman. *Nature in American Literature: Studies in the Modern View of Nature.* New York: Russell and Russell, 1923.

Folsom, Ed, and Cary Nelson. "'Fact Has Two Faces': An Interview with W. S. Merwin." *Iowa Review* 13 (1982): 30–66.

Fox, Matthew. *The Coming of the Cosmic Christ: The Healing of Mother Earth and the Birth of a Global Renaissance.* San Francisco: Harper, 1988.

———. *Original Blessing.* Santa Fe: Bear, 1983.

Franklin, Wayne, and Michael Steiner. "Taking Place: Toward a Regrounding of American Studies." *Mapping American Culture.* Ed. Wayne Franklin and Michael Steiner. Iowa City: U of Iowa P, 1992. 3–23.

Frazier, Jane. *From Origin to Ecology: Nature and the Poetry of W. S. Merwin.* Madison, NJ: Fairleigh Dickinson UP, 1999.

Fritzell, Peter. *Nature Writing and America: Essays upon a Cultural Type.* Ames: Iowa State UP, 1990.

Fromm, Erich. *The Anatomy of Human Destructiveness.* New York: Holt, Rinehart, and Winston, 1973.

Gamble, David E. "Wendell Berry: The Mad Farmer and Wilderness." *Kentucky Review* 2 (1988): 40–52.

Gans, Herbert J. *The Urban Villagers.* New York: Free Press, 1962.

Geertz, Clifford. Afterword. *Senses of Place.* Ed. Steven Feld and Keith H. Basso. Santa Fe: School of American Research Press, 1996. 259–262.

Gelpi, Albert. *A Coherent Splendor: The American Poetic Renaissance, 1910–1950.* Cambridge: Cambridge UP, 1987.

Gelpi, Barbara Charlesworth, and Albert Gelpi, eds. *Adrienne Rich's Poetry and Prose.* New York: Norton, 1993.

Gifford, Terry. *Green Voices: Understanding Contemporary Nature Poetry.* Manchester: Manchester UP, 1995.

Gilcrest, David. *Greening the Lyre: Environmental Poetics and Ethics.* Reno: U of Nevada P, 2002.

Glotfelty, Cheryll, and Harold Fromm, eds. *The Ecocriticism Reader: Landmarks in Literary Ecology.* Athens: U of Georgia P, 1996.

Goodman, Jenny. "Politics and the Personal Lyric in the Poetry of Joy Harjo and C. D. Wright." *MELUS* 19.2 (Summer 1994): 35–56.

Graham, Vicki. "'Into the Body of Another': Mary Oliver and the Poetics of Becoming Other." *Papers on Language and Literature* 30 (1994): 352–372.

Graves, John. *Goodbye to a River.* New York: Knopf, 1960.

Gussow, Alan. *A Sense of Place: The Artist and the American Land.* 1971 reprint. Washington, DC: Island Press, 1997.

Guy, Sandra M. "W. S. Merwin and the Primordial Elements: Mapping the Journey to Mythic Consciousness." *Midwest Quarterly* 38.4 (Summer 1997): 414.

Hall, Donald. *A Roof of Tiger Lilies.* London: A. Deutsch, 1964.

Hall, Edward. *The Silent Language.* New York: Doubleday, 1959.

Harjo, Joy. "Ancestral Voices." Interview with Bill Moyers. *The Spiral of Memory.* Ed. Laura Coltelli. Ann Arbor: U of Michigan P, 1996. 36–49.

———. "The Circular Dream." Interview by Laura Coltelli. *The Spiral of Memory.* Ed. Laura Coltelli. Ann Arbor: U of Michigan P, 1996. 60–74.

———. "Horses, Poetry, and Music." Interview with Carol H. Grimes. *The Spiral of Memory.* Ed. Laura Coltelli. Ann Arbor: U of Michigan P, 1996. 88–98.

———. *How We Became Human.* New York: Norton, 2002.

———. "In Love and War and Music." Interview with Marilyn Kallet. *The Spiral of Memory.* Ed. Laura Coltelli. Ann Arbor: U of Michigan P, 1996. 111–123.

———. *In Mad Love and War.* Middletown, CT: Wesleyan UP, 1990.

———. "Landscape and the Place Inside." Interview with Sharyn Stever. *The Spiral of Memory.* Ed. Laura Coltelli. Ann Arbor: U of Michigan P, 1996. 75–87.

———. "A Laughter of Absolute Sanity." Interview with Angels Carabi. *The Spiral of Memory.* Ed. Laura Coltelli. Ann Arbor: U of Michigan P, 1996. 133–142.

———. *A Map to the Next World.* New York: Norton, 2000.

———. "Ordinary Spirit." *I Tell You Now: Autobiographical Essays by Native American Writers.* Ed. Brian Swann and Arnold Krupat. Lincoln: U of Nebraska P, 1987. 263–270.

———. *She Had Some Horses.* New York: Thunder's Mouth Press, 1983, 1997.

———. "The Spectrum of Other Languages." Interview with Bill Aull, et al. *The Spiral of Memory.* Ed. Laura Coltelli. Ann Arbor: U of Michigan P, 1996. 99–110.

———. "The Story of All Our Survival." Interview with Joseph Bruchac. *The Spiral of Memory.* Ed. Laura Coltelli. Ann Arbor: U of Michigan P, 1996. 20–35.

———. "Weaving Stories for Food." Interview with Donelle R. Ruwe. *The Spiral of Memory.* Ed. Laura Coltelli. Ann Arbor: U of Michigan P, 1996. 124–132.

———. *What Moon Drove Me to This?* New York: I. Reed, 1979.

———. *The Woman Who Fell from the Sky.* New York: Norton, 1994.

———. "Writing with the Sun." *Where We Stand: Women Poets on Literary Tradition.* Ed. Sharon Bryan. New York: Norton, 1993. 70–74.

Harjo, Joy, and Stephen Strom. *Secrets from the Center of the World.* Tucson: Sun Tracks and U of Arizona P, 1989.

Hart, George. "The Poetics of Postmodernist and Neoromantic Nature Poetry." PhD diss., Stanford University, 1997.

———. "Wendell Berry." *Twentieth-Century Nature Writers: Prose. Dictionary of Literary Biography.* Ed. Roger Thompson and J. Scott Bryson. Columbia, SC: BCL, 2002. 48–64.

Heany, Seamus. "The Sense of Place." *Preoccupations: Selected Prose, 1968–1978.* London: Faber and Faber, 1980. 131–149.

Heidegger, Martin. "Building Dwelling Thinking." *Martin Heidegger: Basic Writings.* Ed. David Farrell Krell. New York: Harper and Row, 1977. 347–363.

Hobson, Geary, ed. *The Remembered Earth: An Anthology of Contemporary Native American Literature.* Albuquerque: U of New Mexico P, 1980.

Holmes, Kristine. "'This Woman Can Cross Any Line': Feminist Tricksters in the Works of Nora Naranjo-Morse and Joy Harjo." *Studies in American Indian Literatures* 7.1 (Spring 1995): 45–63.

Hosmer, Robert. Review of *New and Selected Poems,* by Mary Oliver. *Southern Review* 30.3 (1994): 631–640.

Howard, Richard. *Alone with America: Essays on the Art of Poetry in the United States since 1950.* New York: Atheneum, 1971.

Jahner, Elaine A. "Knowing All the Way Down to Fire." *Feminist Measures: Soundings in Poetry and Theory.* Ed. Lynn Keller and Christanne Miller. Ann Arbor: U of Michigan P, 1994. 163–183.

Jeffers, Robinson. *Selected Poems.* New York: Vintage, 1965.

Johnson, William C. "Tangible Mystery in the Poetry of Wendell Berry." *Wendell Berry.* Ed. Paul Merchant. Lewistown, OH: Confluence, 1991. 184–190.

Jonas, Hans. *The Phenomenon of Life: Toward a Philosophical Biology.* Chicago: Humanities Press, 1982.

Keller, Evelyn Fox. *Reflections on Gender and Science.* New Haven: Yale UP, 1985.

Killingworth, M. Jimmie, and Jaqueline S. Palmer, eds. *Ecospeak: Rhetoric and Environmental Politics in America.* Carbondale: Southern Illinois UP, 1992.

Kitchen, Judith. "The Woods Around It." Review of *New and Selected Poems,* by Mary Oliver. *Georgia Review* 47.1 (1993): 145–159.

Knott, John R. "Into the Woods with Wendell Berry." *Essays in Literature* 23.1 (Spring 1996): 124–140.

Kroeber, Karl. *Ecological Literary Criticism: Romantic Imagining and the Biology of Mind.* New York: Columbia UP, 1994.

Krupat, Arnold. "The Dialogue of Silko's *Storyteller.*" *Narrative Chance: Postmodern Discourse on Native American Indian Literatures.* Ed. Gerald Vizenor. 1989. Norman: U of Oklahoma P, 1993. 55–68.

Kubrin, David. "How Sir Isaac Newton Helped Restore Law 'n Order to the West." *Liberation Magazine* 16.10 (March 1972): 32–41.

Kuhn, Sherman M. *Middle English Dictionary.* Ann Arbor: U of Michigan P, 1978.

Kumin, Maxine. "Intimations of Mortality." *Women's Review of Books* 10.7 (April 1993): 19.

LaChapelle, Dolores. *Sacred Land, Sacred Sex—Rapture of the Deep: Concerning Deep Ecology and Celebrating Life*. Silverton, CO: Finn Hill Arts, 1988.

Landow, George P. "Ruskin's Discussion of the Pathetic Fallacy." www.victorian-web.org/technique/pathfall.html

Lang, John. "'Close Mystery': Wendell Berry's Poetry of Incarnation." *Renascence* 35 (1982): 258–268.

Lang, Nancy. "Through Landscape toward Story / Through Story toward Landscape: A Study of Four Native American Women Poets." PhD diss., Indiana University of Pennsylvania, 1991.

———. "'Twin Gods Bending Over': Joy Harjo and Poetic Memory." *MELUS* 18.3 (Fall 1993): 41–49.

Langbaum, Robert. "The New Nature Poetry." *American Scholar* 28.3 (Summer 1959): 323–340. Reprinted in Langbaum, Robert. *The Modern Spirit: Essays on the Continuity of Nineteenth- and Twentieth-Century Literature*. New York: Oxford UP, 1970. 101–126.

Laskowski, Timothy. "Naming Reality in Native American and Eastern European Literatures." *MELUS* 19.3 (Fall 1994): 37–59.

Leen, Mary. "An Art of Saying: Joy Harjo's Poetry and the Survival of Storytelling." *American Indian Quarterly* 19.1 (Winter 1995): 1–16.

Leopold, Aldo. *Sand County Almanac: And Sketches Here and There*. New York: Oxford UP, 1949.

Levertov, Denise. *The Jacob's Ladder*. London: Cape, 1965.

———. *The Life Around Us: Selected Poems on Nature*. New York: New Directions, 1997.

Lewis, C. S. *Studies in Words*. 2nd ed. London: Cambridge UP, 1967.

Lorenz, Konrad. *Studies in Animal and Human Behavior*. 2 vols. Cambridge: Harvard UP, 1970, 1971.

Lovelock, James. *Gaia: A New Look at Life on Earth*. New York: Norton, 1988.

Ludlow, Jeannie. "Working (In) the In-Between: Poetry, Criticism, Interrogation, and Interruption." *Studies in American Indian Literatures* 6.1 (1994): 24–42.

Luke, Timothy W. "On Environmentality: Geo-Power and Eco-Knowledge in the Discourses of Contemporary Environmentalism." *Cultural Critique* 31 (Fall 1995): 57–81.

Lutwack, Leonard. *The Role of Place in Literature*. Syracuse: Syracuse UP, 1984.

Manes, Christopher. "Nature and Silence." *The Ecocriticism Reader: Landmarks in Literary Ecology*. Ed. Cheryll Glotfelty and Harold Fromm. Athens: U of Georgia P, 1996. 15–29.

Martin, Calvin, ed. *The American Indian and the Problem of History*. New York: Oxford UP, 1987.

Marx, Leo. *The Machine in the Garden: Technology and the Pastoral Ideal in America*. New York: Oxford UP, 1964.

McDowell, Michael J. "The Bakhtinian Road to Ecological Insight." *The Ecocriticism Reader: Landmarks in Literary Ecology.* Ed. Cheryll Glotfelty and Harold Fromm. Athens: U of Georgia P, 1996. 371–391.

McGann, Jerome. *The Romantic Ideology.* Chicago: U of Chicago P, 1991.

McNew, Janet. "Mary Oliver and the Tradition of Romantic Nature Poetry." *Contemporary Literature* 30.1 (1989): 59–76.

Meeker, Joseph W. *The Comedy of Survival: Studies in Literary Ecology.* New York: Scribner's, 1972.

Merchant, Carolyn. *The Death of Nature: Women, Ecology, and the Scientific Revolution.* New York: Harper and Row, 1980.

———. *Radical Ecology: The Search for a Livable World.* New York: Routledge, 1992.

Merchant, Paul, ed. *Wendell Berry.* Lewistown, OH: Confluence, 1991.

Merrill, Christopher. *The Forgotten Language: Contemporary Poets and Nature.* Salt Lake City: Peregrine Smith, 1991.

Merwin, W. S. " 'Fact Has Two Faces': Interview." Interview by Ed Folsom and Cary Nelson. *Regions of Memory: Uncollected Prose, 1949–82.* Ed. Ed Folsom and Cary Nelson. Urbana: U of Illinois P, 1987. 335–336.

———. *The First Four Books of Poems: A Mask for Janus, The Dancing Bears, Green with Beasts, The Drunk in the Furnace.* New York: Atheneum, 1975.

———. "An Interview with W. S. Merwin." Interview by David L. Elliott. *Contemporary Literature* 39 (Spring 1998): 6.

———. "Possibilities of the Unknown: Conversations with W. S. Merwin." Interview by Jack Myers and Michael Simms. *Southwest Review* 2 (Spring 1983): 168.

———. *The Pupil.* New York: Knopf, 2002.

———. *The Second Four Books of Poems: The Moving Target, The Lice, The Carrier of Ladders, Writings to an Unfinished Accompaniment.* Port Townsend, WA: Copper Canyon, 1993.

———. *The Rain in the Trees.* New York: Knopf, 1992.

———. *The River Sound.* New York: Knopf, 1999.

———. *Selected Poems.* New York: Atheneum, 1988.

———. " 'This *Absolutely* Matters': An Interview with W. S. Merwin." Interview by J. Scott Bryson and Tony Brusate. *Limestone* 6.1 (1998): 1–8.

———. *Travels.* New York: Knopf, 1993.

———. *The Vixen.* New York: Knopf, 1996.

———. "W. S. Merwin: An Interview." Interview by Michael Clifton. *American Poetry Review* 4 (July–August 1983): 22.

Molotch, Harvey. "L.A. as Design Product: How Art Works in a Regional Economy." *The City: Los Angeles and Urban Theory at the End of the Twentieth Century.* Ed. Allen J. Scott and Edward W. Soja. Berkeley: U of California P, 1996.

Moore, Bryan L. "Robinson Jeffers and the Tragedy of Anthropocentrism." *English Language Notes* 40.3 (March 2003): 58–62.

Murphy, Patrick D. *Farther Afield in the Study of Nature-Oriented Literature.* Charlottesville: UP of Virginia, 2000.

———. *Literature, Nature, and Other: Ecofeminist Critiques.* Albany: State U of New York P, 1995.

———. *A Place for Wayfaring: The Poetry and Prose of Gary Snyder.* Corvallis: U of Oregon State P, 2000.

———. *Understanding Gary Snyder.* U of South Carolina P, 1992.

Murphy, Patrick D., Terry Gifford, and Katsunori Yamazato, eds. *Literature of Nature: An International Sourcebook.* Chicago: Fitzroy Dearborn Publishers, 1998.

Nabokov, Peter. "Present Memories, Past History." *The American Indian and the Problem of History.* Ed. Calvin Martin. New York: Oxford UP, 1987. 144–155.

Nash, Roderick Frazier. *Wilderness and the American Mind.* 3rd ed. New Haven: Yale UP, 1982.

Niehardt, John G. *Black Elk Speaks: Being the Life Story of a Holy Man of the Ogala Sioux.* 1932. Lincoln: U of Nebraska P, 1961.

Nordstrom, Lars. *Theodore Roethke, William Stafford, and Gary Snyder: The Ecological Metaphor as Transformed Regionalism.* Stockholm: Uppsala, 1989.

Oelschlaeger, Max. *The Idea of Wilderness: From Prehistory to the Age of Ecology.* New Haven: Yale UP, 1991.

———. *The Wilderness Condition: Essays on Environment and Civilization.* San Francisco: Sierra Club Books, 1992.

Oliver, Mary. *American Primitive.* Boston: Little, 1983.

———. "Among Wind and Time." *Sierra* (November–December 1991): 33–34.

———. *Blue Pastures.* New York: Harcourt Brace, 1995.

———. *Dream Work.* Boston: Atlantic Monthly P, 1986.

———. *House of Light.* Boston: Beacon P, 1990.

———. *New and Selected Poems.* Boston: Beacon P, 1992.

———. *No Voyage and Other Poems.* Boston: Houghton Mifflin, 1965.

———. *A Poetry Handbook: A Prose Guide to Understanding and Writing Poetry.* San Diego: Harcourt Brace, 1994.

———. *The River Styx, Ohio, and Other Poems.* New York: Harcourt Brace, 1972.

———. *Rules for the Dance: A Handbook for Writing and Reading Metrical Verse.* Boston: Houghton Mifflin, 1998.

———. *Twelve Moons.* Boston: Little Brown, 1979.

———. *West Wind.* Boston: Houghton Mifflin, 1997.

———. *What Do We Know.* New York: Da Capo, 2002.

———. *White Pine.* New York: Harcourt Brace, 1994.

Orr, David. *Earth in Mind: On Education, Environment, and the Human Prospect.* Washington, DC: Island, 1994.

Pack, Robert, and Jay Parini, eds. *Poems for a Small Planet: Contemporary American Nature Poetry.* Hanover, NH: Middlebury College P, 1993.

Parini, Jay. *Theodore Roethke: An American Romantic.* Amherst: U of Massachusetts P, 1979.

Paul, Sherman. *For the Love of the World: Essays on Nature Writers.* Iowa City: U of Iowa P, 1992.

———. "From Here / Now: Mostly on Place." *Witness* 3 (1989): 107–115.

———. "Thinking with Thoreau." *Thoreau Quarterly* 14 (1982): 18–25.

Perkins, David. *A History of Modern Poetry.* Vol. 1, *From the 1890s to the High Modernist Mode.* Cambridge: Harvard UP, 1976.

———. *A History of Modern Poetry.* Vol. 2, *Modernism and After.* Cambridge: Harvard UP, 1987.

Perloff, Marjorie. *The Poetics of Indeterminacy: Rimbaud to Cage.* Princeton: Princeton UP, 1981.

Perreault, Jeanne. "New Dreaming: Joy Harjo, Wendy Rose, Leslie Marmon Silko." *Deferring a Dream: Literary Sub-Versions of the American Columbiad.* Ed. Gert Buelens and Ernst Rudin. Boston: Birkhauser, 1994. 120–136.

Phillips, Dana. "Is Nature Necessary?" *Raritan* 13.3 (Winter 1994): 78–100.

Quetchenbach, Bernard W. *Back from the Far Field: American Nature Poets in the Late Twentieth Century.* Charlottesville: UP of Virginia, 2000.

Rapoport, Amos. "A Critical Look at the Concept of Place." *The Spirit and Power of Place: Human Environment and Sacrality.* Ed. Rana P. B. Singh. Baranasi, India: Banaras Hindu UP, 1993. 31–45.

Rasula, Jed. *This Compost: Ecological Imperatives in American Poetry.* Athens: U of Georgia P, 2002.

Relph, Edward. *Rational Landscapes and Humanistic Geography.* Totowa, NJ: Barnes and Noble, 1981. 161–164.

Rich, Adrienne. *The Fact of a Doorframe: Poems Selected and New, 1950–84.* New York: Norton, 1984.

Ridington, Robin. "Fox and Chickadee." *The American Indian and the Problem of History.* Ed. Calvin Martin. New York: Oxford UP, 1987. 128–135.

Rios, Alberto. Untitled chapter in *Writing the Southwest.* Ed. David King Dunaway. Albuquerque: U of New Mexico P, 1995. 169–174.

Robinson, David M. "Wilderness and the Agrarian Principle: Gary Snyder, Wendell Berry, and the Ethical Definition of the 'Wild.'" *Interdisciplinary Studies of Literature and Environment* 6.1 (Winter 1999): 15–27.

Roethke, Theodore. *The Collected Poems of Theodore Roethke*. New York: Anchor, 1975.

Rogers, Pattiann. *Firekeeper: New and Selected Poems*. Minneapolis: Milkweed, 1994.

Rorty, Richard. *Philosophy and the Mirror of Nature*. Princeton: Princeton UP, 1979.

Rotella, Guy. *Reading and Writing Nature: The Poetry of Robert Frost, Wallace Stevens, Marianne Moore, and Elizabeth Bishop*. Boston: Northeastern UP, 1991.

Ruppert, Jim. "Paula Gunn Allen and Joy Harjo: Closing the Distance between Personal and Mythic Space." *American Indian Quarterly* 7.1 (1983): 27–40.

Sack, Robert D. "Place as Context: The World of Consumption." *Annals of the Association of American Geographers* 78.4 (December 1988): 642–666.

Said, Edward. "Reflections on Exile." *New Worlds of Literature: Writings from America's Many Cultures*. Ed. Jerome Beaty and J. Paul Hunter. New York: Norton, 1994. 101–106.

Sanders, Scott Russell. "Speaking a Word for Nature." *The Ecocriticism Reader: Landmarks in Literary Ecology*. Ed. Cheryll Glotfelty and Harold Fromm. Athens: U of Georgia P, 1996. 182–195.

———. *Staying Put*. Boston: Beacon, 1993.

Sax, Boria. *The Serpent and the Swan*. Granville, OH: McDonald and Woodward Publishing, 1997.

Scarry, John. "Representing Real Worlds: The Evolving Poetry of Joy Harjo." *World Literature Today* 66 (1992): 286–291.

Scheese, Don. "Thoreau's *Journal*: The Creation of a Sacred Place." *Mapping American Culture*. Ed. Wayne Franklin and Michael Steiner. Iowa City: U of Iowa P, 1992. 139–151.

Schweninger, Lee. "Writing Nature: Silko and Native Americans as Nature Writers." *MELUS* 18.2 (Summer 1993): 47–60.

Scigaj, Leonard M. *Sustainable Poetry: Four American Ecopoets*. Lexington: U of Kentucky P, 1999.

Shepard, Paul. *Thinking Animals: Animals and the Development of Human Intelligence*. New York: Viking, 1978.

Silko, Leslie Marmon. "Landscape, History, and the Pueblo Imagination." *The Ecocriticism Reader: Landmarks in Literary Ecology*. Ed. Cheryll Glotfelty and Harold Fromm. Athens: U of Georgia P, 1996. 264-275.

Singh, Rana P. B., ed. *The Spirit and Power of Place: Human Environment and Sacrality*. Baranasi, India: Banaras Hindu UP, 1993.

Slovic, Scott. *Seeking Awareness in American Nature Writing: Henry Thoreau, Annie Dillard, Edward Abbey, Wendell Berry, Barry Lopez*. Salt Lake City: U of Utah P, 1992.

Smith, Patricia Clark, with Paula Gunn Allen. "Earthy Relations, Carnal Knowledge: Southwestern American Indian Women Writers and Landscape." *The Desert Is No Lady: Southwestern Landscapes in Women's Writing and Art.* Ed. Vera Norwood and Janice Monk. New Haven: Yale UP, 1987. 174–196.

Snell, Marilyn Berlin. "The Art of Place: An Interview with Wendell Berry." *New Perspectives Quarterly* 9.2 (1992): 29–34.

Snyder, Gary. *The Back Country.* New York: New Directions, 1967.

———. *Turtle Island.* Boston: Shambhala, 1993.

Stegner, Wallace. "Thoughts in a Dry Land." *Where the Bluebird Sings to the Lemonade Springs.* New York: Random House, 1992. 45–56.

Stevens, Wallace. *The Collected Poems.* New York: Vintage, 1990.

Stitt, Peter. "Tradition and the Innovative Godzilla." *Georgia Review* 39 (Fall 1985): 636–638.

Swenson, May. *Nature: Poems Old and New.* Boston: Houghton Mifflin, 1994.

Teorey, Matthew. "William Wordsworth and Leslie Marmon Silko: Toward an Ecofeminist Future." *Isle: Interdisciplinary Studies in Literature and Environment* 11.1 (Winter 2004): 31–56.

Thevenaz, Pierre. *What Is Phenomenology? Four Basic Essays.* Ed. James M. Edie. Chicago: Quadrangle, 1962.

Thoreau, Henry David. *Collected Poems of Henry Thoreau.* Ed. Carl Bode. Baltimore: Johns Hopkins UP, 1964.

Tuan, Yi-fu. "Place and Culture: Analeptic for Individuality and the World's Indifference." *Mapping American Culture.* Ed. Wayne Franklin and Michael Steiner. Iowa City: U of Iowa P, 1992. 26–49.

———. *Space and Place: The Perspective of Experience.* Saint Paul: U of Minnesota P, 1977.

———. and Gretchen Holstein Schoff. *Two Essays on a Sense of Place.* Madison: Wisconsin Humanities Committee, 1988.

Turner, Frederick. "Cultivating the American Garden." *The Ecocriticism Reader: Landmarks in Literary Ecology.* Ed. Cheryll Glotfelty and Harold Fromm. Athens: U of Georgia P, 1996. 40–51.

———. "On the Revision of Monuments." *The American Indian and the Problem of History.* Ed. Calvin Martin. New York: Oxford UP, 1987. 114–119.

———. *Spirit of Place: The Making of an American Literary Landscape.* San Francisco: Sierra Club Books, 1989.

Vescey, Christopher. "Envision Ourselves Darkly, Imagine Ourselves Richly." *The American Indian and the Problem of History.* Ed. Calvin Martin. New York: Oxford UP, 1987. 120–127.

Voros, Gyorgyi. *Notations of the Wild: Ecology in the Poetry of Wallace Stevens.* Iowa City: U of Iowa P, 1997.

Weekley, Ernest. *An Etymological Dictionary of Modern English*. New York: Dover, 1967.

Weiner, James F. *The Empty Place: Poetry, Space, and Being among the Foi of Papua New Guinea*. Bloomington: U of Indiana P, 1991.

Whithed, Stephen. "On Devotion to the 'Communal Order': Wendell Berry's Record of Fidelity, Interdependence, and Love." *Studies in the Literary Imagination* 27.2 (Fall 1994): 9–28.

Whitman, Walt. *Leaves of Grass and Selected Prose*. 1855. Ed. Sculley Bradley. New York: Holt, Rinehart, and Winston, 1949.

Wiget, Andrew. "Nightriding with Noni Daylight: The Many Horse Songs of Joy Harjo." *Native American Literatures* 1 (1989): 185–196.

Wilson, Alexander. *The Culture of Nature: North American Landscape from Disney to the* Exxon Valdez. Oxford: Blackwell, 1992.

Wilson, Edward O. *Biophilia*. Cambridge: Harvard UP, 1984.

———. "Is Humanity Suicidal?" *Bio Systems* 31.2–3 (1993): 235–242.

Wilson, Peter J. *The Domestication of the Human Species*. New Haven: Yale UP, 1988.

Witherell, Elizabeth Hall. "Thoreau's Watershed Season as a Poet: The Hidden Fruits of the Summer and Fall of 1841." *Studies in the American Renaissance*. Ed. Joel Myerson. Charlottesville: U of Virginia P, 1990. 49–106.

Wood, Douglas Kellogg. *Men against Time: Nicolas Berdyaev, T. S. Eliot, Aldous Huxley, and C. G. Jung*. Lawrence: UP of Kansas, 1982.

Worster, Donald. *Nature's Economy: A History of Ecological Ideas*. Cambridge: Cambridge UP, 1977.

Index